The Money You Inherited

The Money You Inherited

Uncovering—and Rewriting—the Unspoken Beliefs That Shape Your Financial Life

Mira Ellison

Mindful Pages

Published in 2025

ISBN: 9789371779395 (PB)
ISBN: 9789371775137 (eBook)

Published by

Mindful Pages
Imprint of Alpha Editions LLC
312 W. 2nd St #1834
Casper, WY 82601, USA

This book was developed using advanced writing tools to support the drafting and ideation process. All content has been thoughtfully curated, refined, and reviewed to ensure quality and relevance.

Content

Introduction
The Scripts You Didn't Know You Were Following

Long before you ever earned a wage or opened a bank account, you were already learning about money. It was imprinted on you subtly, in the atmosphere of your upbringing. You felt the tension of your parents at month's end. You overheard remarks like "We can't afford that" or "People like us don't live that way." You observed who was praised for saving, who was criticised for spending, and which professions were regarded as respectable or precarious. All of this constituted a kind of psychological inheritance—unwritten, largely unexamined, yet profoundly influential.

This book examines that inheritance. Not the material sort—houses, investments, or debts—but the internalised scripts you received without consent. Scripts that dictate what money means, what it implies about you, what you are permitted to desire or possess, and how safe it feels to have, spend, or want it. These beliefs operate largely beneath conscious awareness, older than any credit score, and more powerful than even the most carefully constructed financial plan. In many ways, they are the hidden authors of your financial life.

You may think your money decisions are logical or rational. Yet how often do you catch yourself repeating patterns you vowed never to follow? Earning well but still anxious. Saving diligently yet feeling guilty for spending. Generous to others yet uneasy receiving. Or achieving apparent success while feeling internally unsettled. The problem is rarely intelligence or discipline—it is the persistence of unexamined scripts.

We inherit these scripts much like we inherit a surname: without choice, often without understanding, and with more influence than we realise. Some emerge from family—a grandmother's caution born of wartime, a father's conviction that money equates to worth, a household where finances were taboo. Others arise from culture: moral coding of wealth and poverty, class-based notions of success, communal norms about giving and saving. And yet others are born of trauma—financial betrayal, childhood scarcity, periods of instability leaving indelible emotional marks.

What unites them is their pre-rational nature. They shape us before we have the cognitive tools to question them. A child observing their parents argue over bills does not reason, "This is a complex interplay of economic stress and relational dynamics." They conclude, "Money causes pain," or "I should never be a burden." These early deductions crystallise into lifelong beliefs, guiding adult behaviours, often unnoticed and unquestioned.

The work of this book is to illuminate these inherited scripts—to trace their origins, reveal how they operate, and explore how they can be consciously rewritten. Unlike manuals on spreadsheets, portfolios, or market timing, this work focuses on the root system underlying financial behaviour: cognition, emotion, identity. It traces habits to beliefs and, crucially, offers a framework for change—through insight, emotional clarity, and behavioural experimentation, rather than sheer willpower.

This is not a guide for financial advice, but for financial awareness. Advice instructs; awareness reveals why you haven't followed it, and what might unfold when you do. Most financial dysfunction is not information scarcity—it is information competing against unexamined belief. You cannot out-budget your unconscious. You cannot invest away shame. You can, however, bring these beliefs into the light, interrogate them, and decide which you wish to carry forward.

Each chapter peels back layers of your psychological architecture. We begin by examining the emotional and cultural inheritance received before you had language to articulate it. We explore the formation of scripts through family, culture, and trauma, and their persistence—not despite change, but often because of it. We analyse the feedback loop between belief and behaviour, showing how it can feel like personality rather than programming. We investigate shame and why financial self-sabotage persists even when knowledge is present.

Later chapters turn toward practice. You will learn to identify your own inherited scripts using techniques drawn from psychology, family systems, and behavioural science. You will examine their origins, their intended purposes, and whether they still serve you. Small, controlled experiments will allow you to test these assumptions—not just in your finances, but in your body, relationships, and self-perception. Composite case studies illustrate these dynamics, offering textured, believable portrayals rather than abstract hypotheticals.

We also explore how money scripts intersect with identity: class, ethnicity, gender, and upbringing shape the moral and emotional meanings attached to wealth. Financial behaviours often serve as proxies for deeper needs: control, safety, self-worth, love. Couples or families clash not because of numbers, but because they operate from differing inherited scripts. Even abundant success does not resolve these tensions; in fact, having "enough" can make them more visible, as necessity no longer masks their influence.

No financial position—whether scarcity or affluence—is immune. Trust-fund heirs may feel inadequate, entrepreneurs may hoard compulsively, high earners may experience persistent fraudulence. These outcomes are not anomalies but natural consequences of unexamined financial scripts. The book aims not merely to enable achievement, but to foster understanding—so that success no longer conflicts with inner peace.

Rewriting these scripts is not linear. There is no final, perfect mindset that dissolves complexity. The goal is coherence: recognising the logic in your contradictions, acting from awareness rather than reaction, and understanding that habits are adaptations, not identity. By discerning which inherited beliefs serve you, you reclaim the capacity to shape your financial life consciously.

Change begins not by denying the past, but by engaging with it. Not by blaming parents, rejecting culture, or discarding personal history, but by evaluating which elements remain useful and which no longer need guidance.

The money you inherited encompasses more than assets; it carries meanings, expectations, fears, and loyalties. Some of it is gold; some a burden. This book offers a careful, intelligent framework for sorting through that inheritance, enabling you, at last, to author your own script.

Chapter 1
Inheritance Isn't Just Material

Long before you ever opened a bank account or received your first payslip, you were already learning about money. Not through formal lessons, but through the ambient cues of daily life—the inflection in a parent's voice when a bill arrived, the pause before a request was granted, the contradictions between what was said and what was done. These impressions were subtle, almost invisible, yet they settled deep in the mind, forming an unconscious template for how money would be understood and navigated in adulthood.

A child quickly learns that money is fraught with tension without anyone ever saying so aloud. They notice the furrowed brow at the checkout, the hurried change of topic, or the grand gestures meant to compensate for what could not be articulated. These early encounters create what might be called implicit financial memory—not concrete knowledge, but emotional understanding; not a plan, but a story. And it is precisely these unspoken narratives that shape adult financial behaviour more than any course, coach, or calculator ever could.

This chapter begins at that point of origin: not with numbers or spreadsheets, but with meaning. The home, the playground, places of worship, and the media we consume all act as classrooms of financial socialisation. But unlike formal education, the curriculum here is inconsistent, ambiguous, and sometimes contradictory. One moment, saving is praised; the next, spending is portrayed as a path to influence or power. One adult worships wealth, another treats it with suspicion. The child pieces together these signals into internal scripts—

rules that seem to explain how money functions and what it means to be "right" with it.

What gives these scripts such power is their emotional dimension. Children don't simply mimic behaviour; they absorb feeling and attach it to future decisions. A parent who saves obsessively may instil not just prudence, but a worldview of scarcity. A household that never discusses finances may convey that transparency is dangerous or shameful. Contradictions—such as simultaneously criticising materialism while celebrating success—can yield potent scripts like "wealth is necessary but impure" or "money invites rejection."

In reality, inherited financial messages form a mosaic. Some tiles are clear, others blurry, some entirely absent. Even silences leave marks. A child in a home where money is never discussed may not remember the details, yet will internalise the unspoken: that money is secret, unapproachable, or forbidden. Financial inheritance, then, is less about explicit teaching than about what is modelled, emotionally charged, or deliberately avoided.

To understand these inherited architectures, it helps to identify their sources, broadly fourfold: family modelling, cultural messages, emotional imprinting, and trauma. Each carries its own methods, weight, and residual impact into adulthood.

Family modelling is immediate and visible. It encompasses parental behaviours, statements, disputes, and responses to scarcity or abundance. Yet even within families, messages are rarely consistent. One parent may champion independence while fostering dependence; another may praise effort while belittling ambition. Such contradictions are human—but left unexamined, they breed internal confusion: adults who simultaneously crave and fear wealth, who seek success but distrust its pursuit, who spend to soothe and save to survive.

Cultural messages frame these family lessons. Norms about success, gendered assumptions about earning, class-based ideas of worth, and media portrayals all contribute. A child raised in 1980s Manchester experiences a different context than one in Silicon Valley during the tech boom, yet both can inherit distorted views: that wealth is unreachable, or conversely, that it is the sole measure of significance. Repeated, subtle, and sometimes polarising, these cues establish assumptions about what is possible, permissible, or desirable.

Emotional imprinting adds yet another layer. Financial events acquire affective weight—a family losing everything in a recession does not merely teach that markets fluctuate; it teaches that security is illusory. A teen showered with gifts during family upheaval may link money with love or guilt. These experiences embed themselves, often persisting despite contradictory evidence. One may intellectually recognise stability, yet the body retains the memory of past instability, guiding decisions more than spreadsheets ever could.

Trauma, while not always dramatic, leaves lasting marks. From systemic poverty to betrayal, from observing caregivers struggle under debt to personal financial failure, trauma encodes scripts with urgency: never let this happen again. These scripts, adaptive in origin, often become rigid and absolutist. Money is danger. Others are untrustworthy. I must manage it all alone. While useful in childhood or crisis, such scripts can distort adult relationships, constrain opportunity, and perpetuate cycles of anxiety.

Psychology offers insight into why these scripts persist. Schema theory suggests the mind creates patterns to interpret experience; attachment theory shows that early relational security shapes financial trust; behavioural conditioning reveals how reward and punishment engrain beliefs. Together, they illustrate how early observation solidifies into adult reality.

The insidious aspect is that inherited scripts feel natural, even virtuous. Once internalised, they cease to read as messages—they read as truth. Unchallenged, they govern quietly but profoundly.

Consider three brief illustrations:

Elena, a corporate lawyer in her forties, struggles to celebrate financial success. Raised where wealth was mocked, she believes visibility invites judgment. Her script: achieve, but remain invisible—manifested in chronic under-sharing, guilt around luxury, and compulsive justification of expenses.

Jordan, a creative entrepreneur, oscillates between financial abundance and rapid spending. His childhood was marked by instability—missed rent, inconsistent income. His script: money disappears quickly, so enjoy it while possible. Beneath the generosity lies distrust of sustainability.

Priya, a high-achieving consultant, overworks and undercharges despite earning well. Her immigrant family equated financial success with struggle. Ease equals laziness. Her script: to deserve wealth, I must endure hardship. The result is burnout disguised as diligence.

None of these patterns are anomalous; they are logical responses to early, potent inputs. While once adaptive, the scripts now operate in contexts where their original logic no longer applies. Yet they remain influential, often unconsciously shaping decisions, behaviours, and self-perception.

The first step to change is recognition. Understanding origins is not about blame, but about reclaiming agency. Not about rejecting the past, but discerning what remains useful and what obstructs growth. Inheritance is not solely a burden; it is also a map. But it must first be acknowledged.

This chapter provides tools to interpret inherited financial scripts, seeing not only what was given or withheld, but what was silently taught. In doing so, it opens the possibility for a more conscious, deliberate relationship with money—where past lessons inform, but do not dictate, the path forward.

The Money You Absorb Before You Understand It

Children learn about money long before they can count it. Even before they grasp what a bank is, or the difference between saving and spending, they are already forming lasting beliefs about financial worth, risk, and security—not through formal lessons, but through emotional exposure. This is not learning in the traditional sense. It is atmospheric absorption. Like moisture in the air, financial attitudes linger invisibly in the household, shaping the child's internal landscape long before conscious thought comes into play. And once absorbed, these early impressions become the foundation upon which adult money behaviours—rational or not—are built.

The assumption that financial literacy begins with education is widely held, but incomplete. Financial identity begins far earlier, not with knowledge but with meaning. It starts when a child notices their parent's tone of voice change when discussing bills. When they hear the sharp silence that follows a declined purchase. When they watch one adult shoulder all the earning responsibility, or another refuse to talk about debt. These interactions are rarely explained; they are *felt*. And what is felt, especially in early childhood, is not forgotten. The emotional tone surrounding money—whether stress, abundance, control, or shame—imprints deeply. Over time, these impressions become scripts: unspoken, often unconscious rules about how money works, what it says about you, and how safe or dangerous it is to have, want, or talk about it.

Children are extraordinary sense-makers. In the absence of explanation, they create their own logic to fill the gaps. A five-year-old who senses anxiety when their parents discuss money doesn't conclude that the global economic system is volatile. They conclude that money is dangerous, or that their needs are a source of burden. A teenager whose requests are consistently denied may internalise that money is always scarce, or that desire itself is indulgent. Conversely, a child rewarded with expensive gifts in place of affection may grow to associate spending with love—or its counterfeit. None of this requires explicit teaching. It happens automatically, through a combination of observation, emotional resonance, and repetition.

What makes these internalisations powerful is their *pre-rational* nature. They are formed before critical thinking, before conceptual nuance, before the ability to challenge or reframe. Because they arrive early, they feel original. We don't experience them as beliefs we inherited; we experience them as truths we discovered. And so, they operate in the background of our lives, influencing financial choices in adulthood without revealing their roots. This is why otherwise intelligent, competent individuals can find themselves stuck in seemingly irrational patterns: compulsive under-earning, money hoarding, chronic overspending, or avoidance of financial conversations altogether. The issue is not willpower. It is programming.

The early emotional environment around money acts as a kind of coding language. And much like a computer running outdated software, we may find ourselves constrained by operating systems we never chose. A child who learns that financial discussions lead to conflict may grow into an adult who avoids talking about money with partners, even when collaboration is essential. A child who sees a parent lose control during periods of financial stress may come to associate money with volatility and fear, prompting a lifelong hyper-vigilance. These behaviours are not always logical, but they are adaptive. They were formed in response to perceived threats—emotional, relational, or existential. And they persist because they once helped the child make sense of their world.

The influence of early financial exposure is compounded by the way children absorb *not just actions, but meanings*. It is not the act of saving that teaches frugality, but the emotional tone attached to it. Saving may be framed as security, or scarcity, or sacrifice, depending on how it is enacted. Similarly, spending may be experienced as freedom, recklessness, joy, or shame. Children learn to read these emotional undercurrents, and the meanings they construct remain long after the behaviours themselves have faded. Two people may grow up in households where spending was frequent, but one associates it with celebration, the other with danger. The difference lies in the meaning attached—not the activity observed.

What's particularly compelling is how *inconsistencies* shape these internalisations just as much as clear patterns. Financial messages are rarely delivered with precision. Most families offer a complex blend of spoken values and unspoken contradictions. A parent may say, "We can't afford that," while driving a luxury vehicle. Another might express disdain for materialism while pressuring their children to out-earn their peers. These mixed messages don't cancel each other out; they create confusion that the child attempts to resolve. The resolution often comes in the form of simplified, emotionally charged scripts: "Money is never enough." "Spending is selfish." "Success means being better than others." These beliefs may not align with reality, but they offer clarity in environments where clarity was lacking.

Over time, these scripts solidify. And because they are rarely interrogated, they become self-fulfilling. A person who unconsciously believes that financial comfort leads to emotional abandonment may sabotage opportunities for stability. Someone raised to believe that money discussions are shameful may avoid financial planning altogether, creating the very insecurity they hoped to prevent. These patterns are rarely connected back to childhood, but that is precisely where their roots lie. The behaviours are downstream; the beliefs, upstream.

This does not mean that early financial exposure determines destiny. But it does shape probability. A household where money was used as a means of control is more likely to produce an adult who sees money as power, not partnership. A family that prized thrift to the point of moral superiority may instil in children the belief that desire is dangerous. A parent's relationship to money—whether anxious, dismissive, obsessed, or avoidant—becomes a mirror that children learn to read, often more closely than the parent reads themselves.

The implications are not purely psychological; they are practical. Many adults seek financial change through external strategies: better jobs, smarter investments, tighter budgets. These are all valuable. But without addressing the early emotional coding, such strategies are often built on unstable ground. Advice doesn't stick if it contradicts a core belief formed in childhood. You can create a beautiful budget, but if your inherited script says "having money makes you a target," you'll find ways to spend it before it accumulates. You can set ambitious goals, but if your emotional template equates wealth with selfishness, you'll find ways to undercut your progress. The deeper work is not technical; it is interpretive. It requires revisiting not just what happened, but *what it meant*—and what it still means today.

This raises a critical distinction between *financial behaviour* and *financial identity*. Behaviour is what we do; identity is who we believe ourselves to be in relation to money. Behaviours can change easily when they're not defending an identity. But when a behaviour is propping up a belief—especially one absorbed early—it resists change. That's why patterns like chronic saving, avoidance of debt, or over-responsibility in financial caregiving can persist even when they are no longer contextually appropriate. The script being defended is deeper than the logic being applied.

Importantly, financial identity is not merely individual. It is often inherited within family systems and reinforced culturally. In collectivist cultures, for example, a child may learn that money should be redistributed within the family network—making independence feel disloyal. In families with intergenerational poverty, messages about survival and self-reliance may take precedence over risk-taking or entrepreneurial thinking. These beliefs are not right or wrong; they are contextual. But unless they are examined, they remain invisible. And what remains invisible cannot be chosen.

None of this is about blaming one's upbringing. The purpose is not to indict parents or caretakers for the beliefs they passed down. Most did so unconsciously, repeating what they had absorbed in turn. The point is to understand the ecology of financial meaning—the layered ways in which early exposure to money attitudes becomes the foundation of adult financial choices. If we want to change those choices, we must understand the soil in which they were planted.

This understanding allows for greater agency. Once we see that a belief is not a truth but a story—crafted early, under conditions we did not control—we can begin to ask different questions. Not "What's wrong with me?" but "Where did this script come from, and is it still serving me?" That shift—from self-judgement to curiosity—is the starting point for genuine transformation.

The child absorbs meanings before they understand money. But the adult can revisit those meanings with new tools, new language, and a new level of psychological maturity. This does not erase the past, but it reframes it. It allows us to distinguish between the wisdom that deserves preservation and the baggage that needs release. Only then can we begin to relate to money not as a legacy to obey, but as a resource to navigate—consciously, flexibly, and freely.

The Four Sources of Financial Scripts

A child who grows up hearing "we can't afford that" learns something about money. But so does the child who hears nothing at all. Silence is not neutral. It is laden with meaning, often more powerful than explicit instruction. In the formation of financial beliefs—what money is, what it means, what it permits, what it endangers—what is said, how it's said, what's done, what's hidden, and what's missing all carry instructional weight. Beliefs are not simply taught; they are transmitted. And the most enduring beliefs are rarely chosen. They are inherited.

The adult who compulsively undercharges for their work is not merely struggling with strategy. The person who hides financial distress until it becomes catastrophic is not simply lacking discipline. These behaviours are expressions of internalised financial scripts—deeply rooted narratives about money, often formed long before the individual had language to describe them. To understand these scripts, one must look beyond behaviour and trace their psychological and emotional sources. Four foundational pillars consistently emerge: family modelling, cultural messaging, emotional imprinting, and trauma. These are not discrete categories; they overlap, reinforce, and at times contradict one another. But together, they form the architecture of financial identity.

Family modelling is the first and most enduring teacher. It is not just what children are told, but what they observe—the rhythm of transactions, the tone of conversations, the emotions tethered to financial acts. When a parent responds to a financial setback with silence and shame, that pattern imprints more deeply than any verbal explanation. The child doesn't need an explicit lecture to internalise a belief. They learn that financial failure is isolating, or that problems must be concealed. If they witness generosity under pressure, they learn that giving is non-negotiable, regardless of cost. If they see one parent dominate financial decisions, they absorb that control over money equals control over others. Family scripts often pass through multiple generations, not because they're rational or effective, but because they are familiar. Repetition feels like truth.

Interestingly, inconsistency can shape beliefs just as potently as repetition. A parent who oscillates between indulgence and deprivation—perhaps splurging on luxuries one month and expressing panic the next—instils confusion that requires resolution. The child, unable to reconcile the paradox, often constructs a simplifying script: "money is unpredictable," or "stability isn't real." These beliefs then guide behaviour, creating adults who either overspend while they can or hoard obsessively against imagined scarcity. The complexity of a parent's financial behaviour becomes distilled into emotionally charged assumptions, and those assumptions—if unexamined—can become lifelong constraints.

Yet not all scripts arise from direct experience. Cultural messaging functions as the broader container in which family narratives unfold. It operates through media, education, religion, politics, and peer dynamics. It tells us who is supposed to have money, what it means to want more, and what success ought to look like. In many Western societies, financial worth is tightly bound to personal worth. To earn is to be competent; to struggle is to be irresponsible. These values may be absorbed passively, but they are not benign. They shape how people judge themselves and others, especially when they fall outside normative patterns.

Consider the subtle, gendered messages embedded in cultural discourse. Boys may be taught to associate money with power and independence, while girls receive implicit lessons linking financial caution to virtue. Ambition in men is celebrated; in women, it is often problematised. Such coding may be less overt today, but its legacy is far from resolved. Similarly, race and class shape expectations in powerful ways. A young person of colour succeeding financially may feel the pressure of representation—carrying the weight of visibility, expectation, and cultural fidelity. For some, financial success becomes a symbol of escape; for others, it raises questions of loyalty or betrayal. Cultural scripts are not merely ideological. They affect whether people feel entitled to prosperity, guilty about it, or suspicious of those who possess it.

While culture and family shape scripts through exposure, emotional imprinting gives those scripts staying power. Specific money-related experiences—especially those charged with emotion—can crystallise into fixed beliefs. A child who feels humiliated for asking for something "unnecessary" may internalise the belief that their desires are indulgent. Someone praised extravagantly for thrift might come to associate restraint with self-worth. These formative experiences often carry more weight than ongoing habits. One intensely emotional incident—being yelled at in a shop, watching a parent panic after losing a job, being shamed for spending a birthday cheque—can encode a narrative that persists for decades.

Imprinting is particularly influential because it bypasses cognition. It is less about logic and more about emotional association. You may know, intellectually, that buying something you enjoy is permissible. But if your nervous system remembers it as dangerous—because it once led to ridicule or regret—you'll hesitate, rationalise, or overcorrect. Emotional memories function as internal weather systems, colouring how you perceive options long after the original event has passed. People do not simply remember experiences; they relive the feelings those experiences evoked. And when money is involved, those feelings often carry moral weight—guilt, pride, anxiety, resentment—all of which shape future decisions.

The final and often least understood source is trauma. Financial trauma is not limited to extreme poverty or catastrophic loss. It includes any moment where financial instability, betrayal, or exposure overwhelmed a person's coping capacity. Trauma distorts not just memory but perception. It narrows attention, heightens threat sensitivity, and creates rigid internal rules for survival. These rules often manifest as extreme scripts: "trust no one with money," "never depend on others," "I must earn to be loved." While such beliefs may have been adaptive in the original context, they become maladaptive when transferred unexamined into different circumstances.

A woman who watched her family lose their home after a parent's failed business may grow up convinced that risk is inherently selfish. Even when she's in a stable, well-resourced environment, that imprint remains. She might pass up opportunities, overwork to avoid imagined collapse, or distrust partners who suggest long-term investment. These behaviours are not conscious choices; they are protective patterns. Trauma scripts don't ask whether conditions have changed. They assume they haven't. And in the absence of deliberate reappraisal, they treat all financial ambiguity as danger.

Equally important is the trauma of absence. Being shielded from financial knowledge can itself be a wound. Many adults recall never learning the basics—how taxes work, what a mortgage is, how to negotiate a salary—because money was deemed too stressful, private, or complex to discuss. The result is not just a knowledge gap but a shame gap. People feel not only underprepared but defective for being underprepared. They do not just lack tools; they question their capacity to learn, trust, or act. This is how silence becomes a script. Not through what it says, but through what it implies: you're not supposed to know this. And that implication becomes a barrier to agency.

These four sources—family, culture, emotion, trauma—are not exhaustive, but they are foundational. They often operate simultaneously, sometimes in harmony, sometimes in tension. A family may promote financial independence while the broader culture valorises collective responsibility. An emotionally imprinted belief in scarcity may clash with cultural narratives of abundance. These contradictions are not flaws; they are features of complex human inheritance. But they require navigation. Scripts are not harmful because they exist. They are harmful when they remain invisible.

What makes financial scripts particularly potent is their disguised authority. They rarely announce themselves as beliefs. They present as instincts, gut feelings, or personal values. This camouflage makes them difficult to question. The man who believes that "real men don't talk about money" is unlikely to see that belief as inherited. He sees it as self-evident, reinforced by culture, emotion, and often peer approval. The woman who believes she must choose between love and wealth doesn't hear it as dogma; she feels it as reality. Until such scripts are surfaced, they continue to guide decisions by default.

Financial scripts do not need to be negative to be limiting. Even seemingly positive beliefs—"save everything," "provide for others," "work hard and rewards will follow"—can become problematic when applied rigidly or out of context. The danger lies not in the content of the script but in its inflexibility. Scripts that cannot evolve are scripts that dictate rather than serve.

Recognising the sources of your financial scripts is not an exercise in blame. It is an exercise in clarity. You are not defective for having absorbed beliefs. You are human. The task is not to erase the past but to understand its influence—to distinguish between beliefs that still reflect your values and those that reflect someone else's fear, unresolved pain, or cultural assumptions. Only then does genuine choice become possible.

Beliefs about money are rarely about money alone. They are about identity, safety, love, worth, and power. To work with them requires depth, patience, and nuance. But the alternative is continuing to be governed by scripts you didn't write, under conditions you no longer live in. That is not intelligence. That is inheritance. And inheritance, while inevitable, is not destiny. What you do with your scripts—once you recognise them—is the beginning of authorship.

The Psychology of Script Formation

By the time most people begin earning, spending, or managing their own money, the core beliefs that will shape how they relate to it are already deeply embedded—long before they are aware those beliefs even exist. These internal frameworks, or financial scripts, rarely begin as conscious conclusions. They take root in childhood through a combination of observed behaviour, emotionally charged experiences, and unspoken but powerfully implied meanings. The mechanisms that embed them are not random; they are rooted in predictable psychological systems. To understand how these beliefs form and become durable, we must look beneath the surface of memory and behaviour into the cognitive architecture that quietly constructs our financial identity. Schema theory, attachment theory, and behavioural conditioning provide a robust lens through which to understand this process. Together, they explain how inherited scripts take hold, why they persist, and what makes them so resistant to change—even in the face of new information.

Schemas are mental frameworks that help us organise and interpret information. They are shortcuts for making sense of a complex world, especially when that world is overwhelming or unpredictable. From infancy, humans begin to develop schemas not just for objects and events, but for relationships, danger, worth, and scarcity. Financial schemas begin forming the moment a child experiences the emotional texture of money in their environment. It may be a parent's anxiety during bill-paying, a fight over spending, or a celebration tied to income. These repeated emotional cues become patterns, and those patterns become expectations: "Money causes stress," "Asking leads to rejection," "Only people like us go without." The child does not analyse these moments; they internalise them. And once a schema forms, it filters future experience. Confirmation bias takes hold. The mind privileges evidence that aligns with the existing schema and disregards that which contradicts it. This is why people can repeat painful financial behaviours—even with contrary data in front of them. The schema was built to create coherence, not accuracy.

These early schemas are rarely about money in isolation. They are entangled with the child's developing sense of self. Who am I, and what am I allowed to have? What is safe to want? What is too much? What will make me loved—or rejected? This is where attachment theory deepens the picture. Early attachment relationships—primarily with caregivers—teach us how the world responds to our needs. Secure attachment develops when caregivers are attuned and responsive. Insecure attachment emerges when responses are inconsistent, neglectful, controlling, or intrusive. Financial scripts often carry the emotional imprint of these early dynamics. A securely attached child who learns that their needs are met reliably may grow up with a healthy sense of entitlement around money: they can ask, receive, and manage resources without shame. Conversely, a child whose needs were ignored or met conditionally may internalise that they must over-function, self-sacrifice, or remain silent to avoid conflict or rejection.

Consider the adult who refuses to ask for a raise despite clear evidence of underpayment. Logically, they know their value. But emotionally, they may carry a script inherited through attachment: "Needing something makes me vulnerable," or

"Asking leads to punishment." These beliefs are not explicitly remembered. They are encoded as *felt realities*. Similarly, a person who compulsively overworks may not simply be ambitious; they may be compensating for a core belief that ease is unsafe or that their worth is conditional on output. The link between attachment and financial behaviour is rarely linear, but it is consistent. When attachment needs are entangled with money—when, for example, love is shown through gifts or financial support is withheld as discipline—the child's developing sense of relational safety fuses with financial meaning. The result is not just a belief about money, but about *deserving*, *belonging*, and *power*.

Layered onto these cognitive and relational patterns is the influence of behavioural conditioning. Classical conditioning (associating a neutral stimulus with a response) and operant conditioning (learning through reward and punishment) play a significant role in reinforcing financial scripts. If a child is praised every time they save and criticised when they spend, they may learn that saving is virtuous and spending is irresponsible—regardless of context. If money is used as a reward for obedience, they may come to see it as conditional and controlling. Conversely, if generosity is consistently met with affection and approval, the child may develop a belief that giving is the primary path to love. These conditioned responses shape not just outward behaviour but internal beliefs about what is acceptable, dangerous, or moral. Because these behaviours are reinforced through emotion—pride, shame, relief, anxiety—they become sticky. The emotional payoff, whether positive or negative, makes the behaviour more likely to repeat.

What makes conditioning particularly insidious in the formation of financial scripts is its capacity to bypass conscious thought. An adult may feel an inexplicable wave of guilt when they consider a luxury purchase—not because they believe luxury is wrong, but because, in their early life, expressions of desire were met with criticism or derision. That guilt is not a rational judgement; it is a conditioned emotional residue. Over time, such responses become automatic. The individual no longer questions the guilt; they adapt around it, shrinking their desires or over-justifying their needs. Similarly, someone who was intermittently rewarded for acts of financial self-sacrifice may become a chronic rescuer in adulthood—absorbing the financial burdens of others while neglecting their own needs. The script reads: "Being needed equals being safe."

Crucially, these systems—schemas, attachment patterns, conditioning—do not operate in isolation. They interact dynamically, often reinforcing one another. A child with an insecure attachment style who experiences inconsistent financial messages will develop both a distorted schema ("money is unstable") and a reinforced behavioural pattern ("I must always be in control"). These beliefs become emotionally charged and neurally reinforced through repetition. They move from situational responses to default modes of engagement. The brain, in service of efficiency, automates what it believes to be true. What begins as a learned response becomes a felt identity. Not "I experienced scarcity," but "I am someone who must prepare for scarcity at all times." Not "My parents controlled money," but "I cannot be financially dependent without losing autonomy." These are not conclusions; they are psychological reflexes.

The persistence of these scripts is partly due to their developmental timing. Scripts that form in early childhood become embedded before the prefrontal cortex—the centre of executive reasoning—is fully developed. That means they are encoded in emotional memory rather than verbal or declarative memory. They are felt rather than thought. This makes them particularly resistant to cognitive challenge. You can explain to someone that they are safe, stable, or deserving, but if their early emotional body was trained to anticipate chaos or deprivation, logic will feel irrelevant. This is why financial scripts often do not respond to information alone.

Budgeting tools, financial planning, or literacy interventions can only go so far when the underlying script treats money as a threat, taboo, or symbol of betrayal.

Moreover, these scripts often become self-reinforcing. Through the mechanism of confirmation bias, people selectively attend to experiences that validate their beliefs and discount those that challenge them. The person who believes "I'm not good with money" will remember the overdraft fees but forget the successful negotiation they pulled off last year. The person who believes "people take advantage of me" will ruminate on every unpaid favour while ignoring moments of genuine reciprocity. This loop between belief and experience can make financial growth feel unattainable—not because change is impossible, but because the belief distorts perception. In psychological terms, the script functions as a *lens*, not a *mirror*. It does not reflect reality; it shapes it.

The role of shame in script formation further complicates the picture. Shame collapses curiosity. It creates urgency without reflection, causing people to act reactively rather than thoughtfully. When financial behaviour becomes a source of shame, it is less likely to be examined. People will hide, rationalise, or double down, rather than question the belief underlying the behaviour. This creates what might be called a "closed script"—a narrative that cannot be challenged because doing so would threaten the self. In these cases, transformation requires not just insight but safety. A person must feel safe enough to hold the discomfort of a new belief, one that contradicts what they have known for decades. This is why script work often mirrors therapeutic work. It is not about correction, but integration—holding the old with compassion while choosing what to carry forward.

Understanding the psychology of script formation is not an academic exercise. It is a practical necessity for anyone seeking to shift entrenched financial behaviours. Without this understanding, people misattribute their struggles to laziness, incompetence, or personal failure. They believe they are undisciplined when they are in fact carrying a lifetime of conditioning. They feel broken when they are simply following an outdated but once-logical emotional blueprint. The goal is not to pathologise these scripts, but to contextualise them. To see them not as flaws but as artefacts—signposts from earlier chapters of life, asking whether they still belong in the story being written now.

The capacity for change lies in awareness. Once a script is seen, it can be named. Once named, it can be questioned. And once questioned, it can be re-authored—not erased, but revised with the maturity, agency, and nuance that adulthood affords. But the first step is understanding not just *that* scripts exist, but *how* they came to be. Because without that understanding, people will continue to blame themselves for behaviours that make perfect psychological sense. And there is nothing more immobilising than mistaking an inherited reflex for a personal failing.

Case Snapshot: Three People, Three Scripts

A financial script rarely announces itself as a belief. It emerges instead as a pattern—a reflexive habit of thought, emotion, or behaviour that feels self-evident, even when it creates friction. Most people don't walk around proclaiming "I believe money ruins relationships" or "I must earn to prove my worth." They feel anxious when discussing money with a partner, or compulsively chase promotions without knowing why. The logic behind these behaviours often remains hidden, coded in experience, emotion, and history. And yet, once made visible, these inherited narratives reveal an inner architecture that is both profoundly personal and surprisingly common. What follows are three compact portraits—fictionalised but psychologically precise—each illuminating how distinct life histories can crystallise into financial scripts that shape adult behaviour in ways that are often invisible to the person living them.

1. Ana: "Money Makes You a Target"

Ana is 38, a successful product manager at a multinational technology firm. She earns well, lives below her means, and has amassed significant savings. On paper, she's financially secure. Yet Ana is perpetually on guard. She declines invitations that hint at lavish spending, avoids discussing her salary even with close friends, and experiences an intense discomfort whenever she feels visible in her success. Her wardrobe is neutral, her car understated, her home sparse. Asked about her financial goals, Ana becomes vague, often pivoting to how "things can change at any time."

What Ana doesn't consciously connect is that her relationship to money is shaped by a formative fear of exposure. Raised in a working-class neighbourhood by immigrant parents who operated a cash-in-hand business, Ana learned early that financial visibility brought scrutiny—sometimes from neighbours, sometimes from family, and occasionally from authorities. Her parents rarely discussed money in front of her, but when they did, the tone was hushed, anxious. She recalls one occasion when a distant relative was accused of flaunting wealth and later robbed. No one drew a direct link, but the implication lingered: *those who show, suffer.*

Over time, Ana developed a script that success must be concealed to remain safe. It wasn't enough to be modest; she had to be invisible. She often turns down deserved promotions if they come with public recognition. She has never negotiated a raise, even though she's been advised to. Her belief—*money makes you a target*—is not illogical in its original context. It protected her family from envy, risk, and judgment. But as an adult operating in a different environment, the script undermines her agency. She has the competence and the resources, but the inherited narrative curtails her expression. The reward for her success remains internalised, never enjoyed.

2. David: "I Have to Out-Earn My Worth"

David, 45, is a partner at a prestigious law firm. He earns more than he ever imagined possible when he was growing up, yet nothing ever feels like enough. He works late into the night, checks email obsessively on holidays, and experiences deep unease when he's not being productive. He rarely spends money on himself without guilt, and when he does, he overcompensates with further austerity—skipping meals, cancelling plans, revisiting spreadsheets. Despite his income, he feels perpetually behind, as though his financial identity were built on a crumbling foundation he must constantly rebuild.

David's upbringing was marked by emotional inconsistency. His father, a former military officer, demanded high achievement but gave praise sparingly. His mother, warm but anxious, managed the family budget with a level of control that bordered on obsessive. Money was always just enough—but always conditional. Good grades were rewarded with pocket money; emotional needs were deflected. As a child, David learned that being exceptional earned him temporary approval, while expressing weakness or wanting more risked disapproval. There was no concept of unconditional enoughness. Worth had to be performed.

His adult script—*I have to out-earn my worth*—is an amalgam of emotional conditioning and survival logic. Success doesn't soothe his inner critic; it feeds it. Even when his financial advisor tells him he could retire early, David brushes it off. He isn't chasing a number; he's chasing relief from a belief that doesn't yield. The more he earns, the more he feels compelled to prove he deserves it. The script operates like a treadmill: progress never feels like arrival. Even therapy, which he pursued briefly, felt like an indulgence he had not earned.

David's case underscores how financial scripts are often entangled with deeper questions of identity and legitimacy.

For him, money is not the problem—it is the proxy. It's the medium through which he negotiates his sense of worth in a world where internal validation was never enough. And because the script is self-reinforcing, it drives high achievement while diminishing satisfaction. Without intervention, success simply escalates the pressure.

3. Leila: "Money Complicates Love"

Leila, 34, works as a freelance designer. Talented and emotionally astute, she has a loyal client base and a modest but steady income. She shares an apartment with her long-term partner, Sam, who earns considerably more as an engineer. Their relationship is strong in many respects—shared values, emotional intimacy, aligned goals. And yet, when it comes to money, Leila withdraws. She refuses joint accounts, avoids discussions about future finances, and becomes defensive whenever Sam suggests co-investing in something significant. The subject of money introduces a static in their communication that doesn't exist elsewhere.

Leila's financial script formed in the shadow of her parents' tumultuous marriage. Her mother, a brilliant woman who abandoned her career to raise a family, was financially dependent on a husband who alternated between generosity and emotional withholding. Money in their home was transactional: a tool used for affection, control, or retribution, depending on the emotional climate. As a teenager, Leila often witnessed her mother bargaining for basic expenditures or being criticised for spending "his money" on what was deemed unnecessary. Despite the emotional abuse, her mother stayed, citing financial insecurity as the immovable constraint. Leila vowed she would never allow money to be a reason to stay where she didn't want to.

That vow, once protective, has hardened into a script: *money complicates love*. For Leila, financial interdependence feels like risk—not just of imbalance, but of erasure. She fears that joint money will lead to joint control, and that joint control will echo the loss of agency she watched her mother endure. Even though Sam is demonstrably different—supportive, communicative, emotionally mature—the script persists. The rational adult sees the opportunity for partnership; the emotional body sees a trap. And so, Leila withholds—not because she doesn't trust her partner, but because she trusts her script more.

Her resistance is not irrational. It is rooted in lived observation, emotional memory, and a protective impulse. But it constrains her capacity to fully integrate intimacy and financial security. The script helped her feel powerful when power felt scarce. Now, it obstructs the very connection she values most.

These three portraits illuminate how inherited scripts do not merely reflect past circumstances—they *preserve* them. They carry the emotional logic of earlier experiences into contexts where that logic no longer applies. Ana is not in danger, but her body responds as though she is. David has nothing left to prove, but his worth feels conditional. Leila has a healthy relationship, but her instincts are coded by dysfunction. None of these individuals lack intelligence, insight, or resources. What they carry is something far more persistent: *unexamined loyalty to an internal rulebook written in childhood, reinforced by experience, and mistaken for truth.*

To examine a script is not to invalidate its origin. Each of these beliefs served a protective function when it was formed. They offered safety, coherence, or control in environments that felt uncertain or unsafe. But scripts are not permanent truths. They are narratives—often inherited, often unspoken—that can be revised when context changes and awareness grows. What these cases make clear is that financial behaviour is never just about the behaviour itself. It is about meaning, memory, and emotion—interacting silently, often irrationally, but always intelligibly once understood.

To begin surfacing these scripts requires not just analytical thinking but emotional precision. What pattern do I repeat? What feeling precedes it? Where did I first learn this was necessary? These are not casual questions. They are, in many ways, the start of authorship—reclaiming agency not by disowning the past, but by seeing it clearly enough to make new choices. Each script, once understood, becomes less of a law and more of a lens—something that can be looked through *or* taken off. And it's in that choice that financial freedom begins. Not in the numbers, but in the narrative.

Chapter 2
The Invisible Code Behind Financial Behaviour

People do not behave irrationally with money because they lack intelligence, discipline, or moral fibre. Quite the opposite: at some deeper level, these behaviours are perfectly rational—they just don't align with the conscious mind that plans, budgets, and resolves. Turning down a raise, underpricing services, hoarding cash, or avoiding financial help may appear counterproductive, but often they are coherent responses to scripts embedded long before adulthood. These are not random lapses; they are coded messages from earlier experiences, waiting to be decoded. The challenge lies not in better spreadsheets, but in better understanding.

On the surface, financial dysfunction can seem baffling. Why would a high earner live as if resources were scarce? Why ignore debt when repayment is possible? Why gamble savings while claiming to value security? Viewed purely as rational behaviour, these contradictions seem illogical. Introduce the notion of inherited scripts—beliefs forged through experience, culture, and emotional conditioning—and the apparent chaos begins to make sense. What seems inconsistent is often a subtle coherence operating beneath conscious awareness. Lasting change, therefore, does not spring from new habits; it begins with insight.

This chapter examines the interior mechanics of that insight: the invisible code shaping money behaviour, even when it clashes with stated values. Central to this is the script-behaviour loop. Beliefs generate behaviours, which in turn reinforce the beliefs. Over time, the loop becomes self-sustaining. You may believe asking for more pay is greedy and refrain from negotiation; stagnation then confirms that belief. You may fear that comfort invites resentment, so you downplay success, which creates distance in relationships, further confirming the original fear. Eventually, the script ceases to feel theoretical—it becomes identity.

Emotion is what cements the loop. Financial actions are rarely neutral; they carry meaning about safety, control, visibility, or adequacy. Often subconscious, this meaning wields authority in moments of choice. You can read books, hire planners, and follow steps meticulously—and still hesitate, avoid, or self-sabotage. Logic alone cannot override deeply charged emotional patterns.

Conflict often accompanies emotion. A person may value generosity yet feel resentment when giving. They may champion independence yet secretly yearn for care. Such tensions indicate cognitive dissonance: the discomfort when behaviour and belief misalign. In finance, this dissonance manifests as justification or avoidance. Overspending can be rationalised as kindness, while avoiding discussions of money may be framed as modesty. Over time, the mind elaborates defences to protect the underlying belief rather than confront the contradiction.

Left unexamined, dissonance fosters shame. Financial shame is pervasive, subtle, and corrosive. It silences honest reflection, undermines learning, and breeds secrecy. People may avoid bank statements not simply to dodge numbers, but to evade feelings of failure, incompetence, or moral weakness associated with those numbers. Behaviour becomes a mechanism of emotional protection; the stronger the protective reflex, the tighter the grip of the original script.

Many internalise financial struggle as personal inadequacy, assuming the problem is weak discipline or lack of ambition. Yet these surface explanations obscure the underlying architecture. Financial tools cannot rewrite a belief that spending is dangerous or that accumulation invokes guilt. Goal-setting fails when scripts decree that one cannot earn more than one's parents, or that success comes at the expense of love. Behavioural change remains precarious until the belief itself is recognised and addressed.

This explains why conventional advice often falls short. It treats symptoms, not the system. People do not act purely on conscious intent but according to scripts written decades prior. Without surfacing these scripts, attempts at change rely on compliance, not transformation. Habits forced against the grain of belief feel hollow—or collapse under stress, which reactivates the old script.

Consider under-earning. It may seem a confidence issue or market mismatch. Beneath the surface, however, a script might be at play: "I must not outshine my community" or "more money brings unbearable expectations." These are not abstract concepts but deeply felt loyalties, frequently inherited or reinforced early. A client recounted that whenever he contemplated raising rates, his late father's voice echoed: "Don't get too full of yourself." Rate increases became emotional rebellion; self-sabotage looked externally like poor planning but internally was fidelity to identity.

Compulsive saving illustrates another pattern. Praised culturally, it can mask scarcity-driven beliefs that reject abundance. A woman in her fifties, financially secure and child-free, described near panic at spending even a small amount on herself. Her childhood instilled: "security is fleeting—protect it at all costs." Planning could not override the emotional logic that once ensured survival. Numbers told one story; embodied experience told another.

Financial self-sabotage offers yet another lens: behaviours that contradict stated goals. Missing deadlines despite available funds, taking impulsive risks, or undermining stability all seem irrational. Yet, through the script–behaviour loop, they are logical—protecting the integrity of an inherited belief. If your script says "stability is forbidden," instability feels natural. If it says "success isolates," sabotage feels protective. Behaviour is not failure; it is fidelity to an internal narrative.

These mechanisms influence perception as much as action. Two people may endure identical setbacks—say, an investment loss—but interpret them differently. One views it as temporary fluctuation; the other as proof of personal inadequacy. The script dictates meaning, which governs subsequent behaviour. This recursive logic—belief, behaviour, consequence, reinforced belief—sustains itself unless deliberately interrupted.

The aim here is not to pathologise but to illuminate. When money behaviour confounds, it is not irrationality at fault; it is the activation of older, contextually adaptive scripts. The question shifts from "what's wrong with me?" to "which script am I following, and is it fit for my current life?" Curiosity, not blame, initiates clarity.

What follows will explore these hidden codes in depth: how beliefs become behaviour, behaviours crystallise into identity, and dissonance and shame obscure origins. Above all, it will demonstrate why conventional advice—however well-meaning—cannot endure without addressing the psychological framework beneath behaviour. Until the script evolves, patterns persist, and no strategy can outrun a belief that insists you are not meant to succeed.

When Money Doesn't Make Sense

There are few domains in life where the distance between what people know and what they do is as stark—and as misunderstood—as it is in personal finance. People who are competent, educated, even outwardly successful often find themselves paralysed or inconsistent when it comes to money.

They ignore bills until fees accrue. They spend compulsively during periods of stress. They undercharge for their services, even when they resent the consequences. They accumulate savings but struggle to enjoy them. To outsiders—and often to the individuals themselves—these behaviours appear irrational, self-defeating, or undisciplined. But irrationality is rarely the root cause. More often, these behaviours make perfect sense once they are decoded through the lens of hidden beliefs.

What appears as a pattern of dysfunction is often a symptom of an invisible logic. A person avoids financial planning not because they are lazy but because they have internalised the belief that certainty breeds disappointment. Someone may compulsively save not out of prudence but because they were taught, consciously or not, that abundance invites punishment or loss. Another may under-earn or self-sabotage precisely because success would violate a deeper emotional loyalty—to a parent who struggled, to a family that revered modesty, or to a culture that equates financial visibility with arrogance. These are not isolated quirks; they are emotionally charged beliefs encoded in early experience and reinforced through repetition. Once installed, they act like mental software: invisible, automatic, and resistant to contradiction.

Take under-earning, for example. It is often pathologised as a lack of confidence or poor market positioning. But these explanations miss the psychological substrate. A person may under-earn because their inherited script says that money must be tied to hardship. If they grew up watching their parents toil without reward, or if ease was framed as laziness, then earning well without struggle may feel disloyal, even dangerous. Another individual may associate financial advancement with emotional abandonment—perhaps a parent became more absent after receiving a promotion, or success was consistently framed as "selling out." In these cases, under-earning is not a failure; it is a form of emotional regulation. The person is unconsciously avoiding the consequences they associate with visibility or growth.

Compulsive saving, too, often carries an emotional rationale that defies surface logic. A person may have a healthy income, a robust safety net, and no dependents, yet still experience guilt or anxiety every time they spend. They may avoid leisure, delay necessary purchases, or fixate on hypothetical disasters. To others, this may look like responsibility taken too far. But to the individual, it often reflects a deeper belief: that safety is never guaranteed, or that self-nourishment is unjustified unless earned through crisis. These beliefs are not fantasies—they are emotional relics. They were formed in environments where scarcity was real or where resources were tied to moral judgements. Once ingrained, they are difficult to dislodge through logic alone.

Perhaps the most difficult pattern to witness—especially for those who are otherwise high functioning—is financial self-sabotage. This can take many forms: taking unnecessary financial risks just as things stabilise, ignoring clear opportunities for growth, or allowing avoidable mistakes to snowball into larger problems. On the surface, these behaviours look inexplicable. But in many cases, they are driven by a script that equates success with danger or separation. If a person holds the belief—consciously or not—that prosperity leads to isolation, envy, or moral compromise, then the psychological cost of success becomes too high to bear. Self-sabotage becomes a means of returning to emotional congruence. It is not a lack of ambition—it is a defence against perceived threat.

Understanding these behaviours requires a shift in interpretive framework. Conventional financial discourse often assumes that people are primarily motivated by rational cost-benefit analysis. But this assumption collapses in the face of lived experience. Money is not just a medium of exchange; it is a mirror of identity, values, and relational history. When a financial decision feels confusing, contradictory, or extreme, it is often reflecting an internal conflict that logic cannot resolve. People do not act according to what they know; they act according to what they *believe is safe*. And safety, in the emotional sense, is a learned state. It is shaped not by reason but by association, experience, and reinforcement.

This helps explain why financial advice, even when technically sound, so often fails to change behaviour. Telling someone to automate their savings, track their expenses, or renegotiate their salary is useful only if those actions do not violate a core belief. If a person believes that receiving more means taking from others, or that planning invites disappointment, then following the advice becomes psychologically incoherent. It generates friction—not because the advice is bad, but because it conflicts with a script that feels more fundamental. And in moments of stress or ambiguity, the script will almost always win.

That's why willpower is an unreliable tool for financial change. Willpower can enforce short-term compliance, but it rarely generates long-term transformation. When a person is working *against* an internal belief, effort becomes exhausting. They can force themselves to budget, negotiate, or invest, but each act feels like a betrayal. Eventually, the tension between behaviour and belief results in fatigue, sabotage, or relapse. It is not that they lack discipline. It is that the behaviour they are trying to adopt feels emotionally unsafe.

These dynamics also help explain why people often behave differently in financial situations that are objectively similar. Two individuals with the same income, background, and goals may take radically different approaches to money. One may treat surplus income as a resource to invest; the other may spend it immediately or give it away. The difference lies not in financial literacy but in the emotional meanings assigned to money. For one person, money may represent freedom; for another, guilt. For one, planning may signal control; for another, fear of disappointment. These meanings are shaped early, often outside awareness, and they become default settings unless intentionally examined.

To interrogate these defaults, a person must first develop the capacity to pause between impulse and action—to ask, not just "what am I doing?" but "what do I believe this action means?" This requires a level of self-observation that most financial education skips entirely. It is not enough to identify the behaviour. One must locate the script that fuels it, understand its origin, and determine whether it still serves a meaningful purpose. Without that inquiry, behavioural change becomes cosmetic at best.

Real-world examples underscore this point. A senior executive repeatedly underbills her time, despite knowing it devalues her expertise. When asked why, she finally admits, "It feels manipulative to charge more for something that comes easily." Her behaviour is not a pricing error; it is a reflection of a belief that value must be effortful. A young man with a stable job refuses to build savings, cycling through small crises that erode his progress. Eventually, he realises that stability feels foreign—and therefore unsafe. He associates routine with stagnation, shaped by watching his parents deteriorate emotionally in the monotony of survival. His lack of savings is not a planning flaw; it is a script of identity.

In these cases, the turning point is never simply a better strategy. It is a new awareness of what is being protected, avoided, or affirmed through the behaviour. This kind of awareness requires not only introspection but compassion. Scripts are not pathology—they are adaptations. They were often formed in environments where the person had limited power, limited information, or limited emotional safety. What now looks like dysfunction may have once been the best available strategy. And that recognition is essential. People cannot release what they still need to justify. They must first honour the script for what it once offered before they can assess whether it is still necessary.

There is a quiet but powerful dignity in this kind of work. It reframes struggle not as failure but as fidelity—to old codes, old loyalties, old meanings. And in that reframing lies the possibility of change. Not superficial change, driven by rules or pressure, but durable change, anchored in understanding. When a person can say, "This behaviour made sense once—but it doesn't make sense now," they are no longer trapped by contradiction. They are no longer reacting to invisible history. They are authoring the next sentence in a script they have finally begun to read.

The Script-Behaviour Loop

People don't repeat financial behaviours simply because they're habits. They repeat them because, at a deep cognitive-emotional level, the behaviour confirms a belief they already hold—often one they don't consciously know they're living by. In this way, beliefs generate behaviours, and those behaviours then become the evidence that reinforces the belief. It is a circular process so seamless and self-validating that it doesn't feel like a loop at all. It feels like truth. Over time, the belief-behaviour pairing becomes internalised as identity: *this is just who I am with money.* But beneath the surface of that apparent personality lies something far more malleable—and more powerful: an inherited script playing itself out through a feedback system that was never consciously chosen.

The term "script" refers to an internalised, often unexamined belief that shapes perception and guides action. These scripts are typically formed early in life, shaped by emotional experiences, relational dynamics, cultural messages, and observed behaviour. For instance, if a child regularly witnessed their parents argue over spending, they might adopt a script like *money causes conflict*. That belief becomes a mental rule, even if it is never articulated. As the child matures, they may avoid financial discussions in adulthood, fearing confrontation or relational tension. The avoidance then perpetuates misunderstanding, secrecy, or inequity in their relationships—outcomes that, in turn, reinforce the original belief that money disrupts harmony. The script initiates behaviour; the behaviour reinforces the script. The loop is complete.

This is not merely a philosophical concept—it is a core mechanism in how human beings make meaning. The brain privileges cognitive consistency over accuracy. Once a belief is established, especially one encoded emotionally, the mind begins filtering new experience through it. This is known as confirmation bias. You notice what supports your preconception and ignore or minimise what contradicts it. When this bias operates within the script-behaviour loop, it becomes a kind of psychological enclosure: the person keeps encountering "evidence" that supports the script, even though they're generating much of that evidence through their own behaviour.

Consider a freelance designer who believes *I'm not worth high rates*. That script may have originated in family dynamics that framed self-promotion as arrogance or discouraged asking for what one needed. As an adult, she underquotes projects or hesitates when discussing money with clients. Those clients respond by undervaluing her work or expecting discounts. Each experience confirms her sense of inadequacy. She sees the result—low earnings—not as a consequence of the script, but as a confirmation of it. The loop is invisible because the belief feels explanatory. And as long as it goes unexamined, the system remains self-sustaining.

Another common example is compulsive financial caretaking—someone who constantly bails others out, pays for group expenses, or takes on financial responsibility well beyond what's expected. The underlying script might be *my value lies in what I provide*, formed in an early environment where affection was conditional or support had to be earned. The adult behaviour—giving beyond capacity—generates appreciation in the short term but often breeds resentment or burnout in the long term. Yet the next time a request arises, they overextend again. Each instance reinforces the script: *if I don't give, I disappear*. The behaviour is not merely habitual—it is evidentiary. The person is living out a belief and collecting experiences that make it feel irrefutable.

This is precisely why financial coaching, planning, or self-help often struggles to deliver lasting change. Without attention to the script, new behaviours feel disconnected, even threatening. A budgeting tool may recommend allocating money for pleasure or rest, but if a person's script equates enjoyment with waste or indulgence, they will override the suggestion or self-sabotage. If someone with a scarcity script starts earning more, they may unconsciously overspend or under-save to return to familiar emotional territory. These are not logical decisions—they are protective ones. And because the behaviour "proves" the belief, the script becomes more deeply embedded.

The script-behaviour loop also has a powerful effect on self-concept. Over time, people begin to conflate the script with their identity. A person who chronically avoids looking at their finances may not say, "I have a script about money being overwhelming." They say, "I'm just bad with money." Someone who undersells themselves isn't likely to identify a childhood script around humility and sacrifice—they'll say, "I'm just not the kind of person who negotiates." This identity formation is not benign. It shapes expectations, limits possibilities, and makes change feel like an existential risk. To adopt a new financial behaviour is to challenge the internal narrative that defines the self.

Importantly, the script-behaviour loop operates regardless of external circumstances. That is what makes it so deceptive. A person may increase their income, change careers, or enter a new relationship—and still find themselves repeating the same dysfunctional patterns. The context has changed; the script has not. A scarcity mindset will recreate scarcity even amid abundance. A control-based script will generate anxiety in situations where flexibility would suffice. Financial growth, without cognitive and emotional integration, often triggers the script more acutely. The stakes feel higher, and the dissonance between the old belief and the new situation becomes more pronounced. This can lead to panic, withdrawal, or unconscious sabotage—all in service of returning to the loop's emotional baseline.

Yet this process is not immutable. What makes the loop feel like fate is its invisibility. Once illuminated, it becomes interruptible. Recognising the script means pausing long enough to name it: *What am I believing right now? Where did that belief come from? What behaviour is it generating? And what result is that behaviour reinforcing?* These questions are deceptively simple, but they demand a level of honesty and self-inquiry that most people aren't taught to apply to their financial lives. The inquiry must be non-judgemental, because shame only deepens the loop. If someone believes *I'm irresponsible*, then judging their overspending only confirms the script. Insight, not criticism, is what disrupts the cycle.

One powerful intervention is behavioural contradiction: intentionally adopting a small, safe action that contradicts the script. A person who believes *I always have to give more than I receive* might practice saying no to a request that feels transactional. The resulting discomfort reveals the strength of the script—but also its malleability. Each new behaviour generates a new experience, and that experience has the potential to revise the belief. This is the inverse of the script-behaviour loop: belief changes behaviour, and behaviour then updates belief. But for that process to begin, the person must be willing to tolerate the dissonance of acting against the old code.

The loop also explains why cognitive insight alone often fails to create change. A person may fully understand that their script is irrational or outdated. They may have talked it through in therapy or journaled about its origin. But if they continue behaving in ways that reinforce it, the emotional system remains convinced. Change does not solidify until experience aligns with the new belief. This is the difference between intellectual awareness and embodied transformation. Knowing the script is a critical step—but living differently is what rewires it.

In financial life, this distinction matters deeply. Because the stakes are not just numerical—they are psychological. Scripts inform how people evaluate risk, interpret feedback, relate to others, and regulate their sense of self. And when scripts are inherited—passed down through generations, cultures, or collective trauma—the behaviours that sustain them feel morally or emotionally justified. Challenging them may not just feel inconvenient; it may feel disloyal or unsafe. That's why self-compassion is not a soft concept here—it's a strategic necessity. Without it, the script wins by default.

The script-behaviour loop, then, is not a flaw in how people operate—it is an elegant survival mechanism. It creates predictability, coherence, and emotional safety. But it does so at a cost: the cost of freedom, agency, and choice. To break the loop is not to disown the past, but to become conscious of its influence—and to decide, with clarity and courage, what patterns are worth preserving and what beliefs are ready to be rewritten. Because what feels like personality is often programming. And what is programmed can, with intention and insight, be re-coded.

Cognitive Dissonance and Financial Shame

It is entirely possible to believe in financial responsibility and still avoid opening your bank statements. To value generosity yet feel resentful every time you give. To view wealth as a marker of success and simultaneously mistrust those who have it. These contradictions are not signs of hypocrisy or confusion; they are psychological fault lines where competing beliefs collide. When a person's financial behaviours run counter to their stated values or identity, the result is *cognitive dissonance*—a state of internal discomfort that the mind instinctively tries to resolve. But in the realm of money, resolution is rarely straightforward. Because more often than not, the tools we use to resolve dissonance—rationalisation, suppression, avoidance—don't solve the problem. They bury it. And what buries it most effectively, and destructively, is shame.

Cognitive dissonance, first articulated by psychologist Leon Festinger in the 1950s, describes the tension that arises when a person holds two or more conflicting beliefs, or behaves in a way that contradicts their beliefs. The mind, seeking coherence, will often resolve the discomfort by adjusting one of the variables—changing the belief, modifying the behaviour, or reframing the contradiction. In financial life, however, this mechanism often gets hijacked by deeper emotional scripts. Rather than confronting the root conflict, people default to justification: *I overspent because I deserved it. I gave too much because I'm just a generous person. I ignored the debt because thinking about it makes me anxious.* These justifications alleviate the discomfort momentarily, but they don't address the structural cause. The deeper the contradiction, the more sophisticated the justifications become—and the more the dissonance hardens into shame.

What makes financial dissonance uniquely potent is that money is not just practical; it is symbolic. Financial choices often carry implications about identity, morality, and belonging. To spend impulsively might not just violate a budgeting rule—it might clash with one's belief in being disciplined. To avoid saving could be interpreted not simply as poor planning, but as irresponsibility. And because these meanings are rarely discussed openly, the conflict becomes internalised. People begin to experience themselves not just as people who *did* something questionable, but as people who *are* questionable. This is the domain of shame, and it is where financial dissonance becomes corrosive.

Shame differs from guilt in one critical respect. Guilt is about actions—*I did something wrong*. Shame is about identity—*I am wrong*. When shame attaches itself to money, it distorts not only behaviour but self-perception. A person who misses a credit card payment doesn't just feel frustrated; they feel unworthy. Someone who grows up in poverty and later earns well might still feel fraudulent, as if success doesn't quite belong to them. The shame doesn't always come from the behaviour itself, but from the *incongruence* between the behaviour and the internalised ideal. The more someone values financial competence, the more intense the shame when they act against it.

This dynamic often plays out in highly intelligent, capable individuals who hold themselves to high standards. They believe in responsibility, discipline, and rational decision-making—yet they find themselves procrastinating on taxes, ignoring mounting debt, or failing to set financial boundaries. The resulting dissonance is not just cognitive—it's moral. The behaviour contradicts not only what they *know*, but who they believe they're *supposed to be*. That rupture triggers shame, and the shame, in turn, drives further avoidance. The person hides the evidence, withdraws from conversation, and pretends the problem is smaller than it is. But beneath the surface, the shame deepens. The internal monologue becomes punitive: *How could I let this happen? What's wrong with me? Why can't I get it together?* At that point, the original dissonance has metastasised into self-reproach.

This is not a function of weakness or ignorance. It is a function of unintegrated belief. Most financial dissonance arises from a misalignment between surface values and underlying scripts. For example, someone may consciously believe in financial independence, but carry a deeper inherited script that says *being taken care of is love.* When they try to assert financial autonomy—refusing help, making their own investments—they experience dissonance. The conscious mind applauds the decision, but the unconscious registers it as abandonment or betrayal. If they cave and accept help, the dissonance resolves—but shame sets in: *I said I was independent, but I'm not.* The cycle continues.

Another example: a person believes in generosity, but grew up in an environment where resources were scarce and giving was often punished or guilt-ridden. As an adult, they want to be generous—but every act of giving triggers anxiety. If they hold back, they feel stingy; if they give, they feel exposed. Whatever they choose, it doesn't sit cleanly. Over time, the tension becomes habitual. They begin to avoid situations where they might be asked for support. They rationalise their withholding. They feel guilty but unable to change. The outward behaviour appears inconsistent. But internally, it's a complex negotiation between competing loyalties.

Financial shame also thrives in the space between appearance and reality. People feel pressure to project competence, even when their internal state contradicts it. They may keep up appearances—polished clothing, generous hospitality, professional success—while hiding financial confusion or debt. This performance, while socially rewarded, deepens the dissonance. The gap between image and experience becomes harder to reconcile. And when the mask slips, the shame rushes in—not only about the numbers themselves, but about the perceived deception: *Everyone thinks I'm doing well. If they knew the truth, they'd think I'm a fraud.*

In professional environments, this tension is especially acute. Financial literacy is assumed among high achievers, but rarely taught. People who excel in technical or creative fields may find financial planning baffling or emotionally overwhelming, but feel unable to admit it. They nod along in investment discussions, outsource key decisions, or avoid asking questions. The dissonance lies between their actual competence and their perceived incompetence. Rather than confront the gap, many retreat. The result is a financial life built on fragmentation—competent in some areas, deeply anxious in others, with no safe place to integrate the whole.

Cognitive dissonance becomes particularly entrenched when paired with legacy shame—beliefs inherited from parents, community, or culture. A person may carry shame not just about what they do, but about *where they came from*. If money was a source of chaos, secrecy, or moral judgement in their upbringing, they may have absorbed the idea that financial clarity is reserved for others—more disciplined, more deserving, more stable. When they make progress, the dissonance can intensify. Success feels incongruent with the inherited identity. Some pull back. Others hide their progress. Still others sabotage it, not out of incompetence, but out of unconscious loyalty to a version of themselves that feels more real.

The antidote to this cycle is not perfection. It is integration. People cannot eliminate dissonance through performance, nor can they resolve shame by doing better. The work begins with *naming* the contradiction without judgement. To say, "I value financial transparency, and I've been avoiding hard conversations," is not weakness. It is clarity. To say, "I feel shame about my spending, and I don't yet know how to change it," is not failure. It is precision. Shame thrives in ambiguity. Once the dissonance is mapped—belief versus behaviour, ideal versus reality—the charge begins to loosen.

This requires emotional maturity and intellectual honesty. It asks the person to locate not just what they're doing, but *why* they're doing it—and where that why came from. Did it begin with a childhood message? A cultural norm? A traumatic moment that coded safety into avoidance? The goal is not to justify the behaviour, but to understand its origin. Because once the behaviour is understood, it becomes optional. And once the shame is named, it begins to dissolve.

None of this work is linear, and none of it is about arriving at a flawless financial life. It is about recognising that contradiction is not pathology—it is information. Dissonance points to tension. Shame points to meaning. When treated with care, both become access points for deeper understanding. The person who can face these internal fractures without collapsing into self-blame is not only more financially coherent—they are more free. Because the problem was never the behaviour. It was the silence around the script that made the behaviour feel inevitable. And that silence—once broken—cannot hold power.

Why Advice Doesn't Stick

Most people know what they're supposed to do with money. Spend less than you earn. Save for emergencies. Invest early. Avoid high-interest debt. These principles are simple, clear, and widely available—repeated in podcasts, plastered across financial blogs, distilled into viral charts and budgeting apps. And yet, adherence to this basic advice remains staggeringly inconsistent. People set savings goals they don't follow through on, abandon their budgets within weeks, forget their login details for the apps they downloaded in good faith. Even highly educated, motivated individuals struggle to sustain what they intellectually know to be sound financial practices. The failure isn't a matter of logic or literacy. It is a matter of *fit*—between the advice offered and the internal world of the person receiving it.

Financial advice assumes that behaviour change is a matter of information and willpower. If you know what to do and want to do it badly enough, you will. But this assumption collapses under scrutiny. If knowledge were sufficient, most financial planners would be out of business. The real problem isn't that people lack access to good advice—it's that *the advice is landing on terrain it doesn't recognise*. That terrain is the person's inherited financial scripts: the unconscious beliefs, emotional associations, and internalised expectations that govern how they relate to money. Unless those scripts are made visible and engaged with directly, new advice simply gets absorbed into the architecture of the old beliefs. It may feel inspiring in the moment, but it doesn't change the operating system.

Take the example of budgeting. At its core, budgeting is just maths: track what you earn, allocate what you spend, correct the gaps. But in practice, budgeting often triggers intense emotional responses—shame, overwhelm, avoidance, defiance. Why? Because for many people, budgeting is not a neutral act. It is a confrontation with scarcity, a reminder of failure, or a perceived loss of freedom. If someone grew up in a household where budgeting meant deprivation, conflict, or guilt, they may resist it instinctively. No amount of logic or spreadsheet optimisation will override the visceral association. The advice may be valid, but the experience of following it feels intolerable. So it is dropped.

Similarly, advice to "just automate your savings" presumes that the obstacle is a logistical one. But what if the person associates saving with hoarding, or with withholding love? What if they were raised in a family where generosity was equated with spontaneous giving, and saving felt cold or selfish? The instruction clashes not with reason, but with identity. In such cases, saving will provoke internal tension, and any behaviour that causes identity-based discomfort is unlikely to be sustained. The same goes for debt repayment, spending boundaries, or investment strategies. If the advice disrupts the person's underlying narrative of who they are—or who they believe they must be—it will be resisted, quietly or overtly, until the narrative itself is re-examined.

This is why financial advice often fails not at the level of execution, but at the level of interpretation. People don't just hear advice—they filter it through their worldview. A suggestion that sounds empowering to one person may sound condescending to another. A plan that feels clear to one may feel impossible to another, even if their external circumstances are similar. The difference lies in the *internal conditions* the advice is entering: the emotional schema, cognitive associations, and behavioural defaults shaped by past experience.

Modern behavioural science has given us countless tools to nudge financial behaviour—default settings, habit trackers, commitment devices. These can be helpful, but they work best when they complement an existing belief system. When they challenge a core script, they may fail or even backfire. For example, someone who holds the unconscious belief *"I'm not good with money"* may use a budgeting app religiously for two weeks, then miss a day, feel like a failure, and delete the app altogether. The advice wasn't wrong. But it didn't address the identity wound that made failure intolerable.

Another problem with conventional advice is its reliance on abstract universality. It treats the user as a generic rational actor, rather than a meaning-making individual shaped by culture, memory, and emotion. Advice such as "build a six-month emergency fund" or "contribute to your pension before anything else" may make perfect economic sense, but if someone comes from a background where money was always for immediate survival, deferred gratification can feel risky rather than wise. Their nervous system has been trained to prioritise short-term safety. Asking them to prioritise future security without engaging that history is like handing them a ladder and ignoring that they're standing in quicksand.

This misalignment is further complicated by the moral undertones baked into much financial advice. Words like "discipline," "freedom," "success," and "security" are loaded with cultural assumptions. For someone raised in a household where financial control was used as a tool of domination, being told to "be more disciplined" can sound less like guidance and more like a revival of old wounds. Advice that centres discipline without examining its emotional connotations may be interpreted as shaming, even if well-intended. In the same vein, praise for financial independence can sound hollow or unrealistic to those whose familial scripts emphasised dependence, communal obligation, or sacrificial giving.

The deeper issue is that much of the financial advice industry rests on a model of *compliance* rather than *curiosity*. It assumes that the user must adapt to the tool, rather than the tool adapting to the user's lived reality. This can be seen in the language of many apps and financial products—track, monitor, control, eliminate, optimise. These are managerial verbs. They assume the person is a system to be tweaked. But human behaviour is not a spreadsheet. It is a complex, emotionally-saturated process that must be approached with nuance, not algorithms.

This is not an argument against advice, but for *contextualised* advice—advice that takes seriously the inner world of the person receiving it. The most effective financial guidance begins not with the question *What should I do?*, but *What do I believe?* Only then can the advice be assessed for compatibility. A person who understands their scripts can evaluate advice more critically: *Does this strategy align with the kind of financial identity I want to build? Does it support or contradict the stories I carry from my past? Will following it reinforce a belief I'm trying to outgrow?* These questions create space for discernment and integration—two qualities sorely missing from the conventional advice model.

Willpower alone is a notoriously unreliable engine for change. Research consistently shows that people revert to their baseline patterns unless those patterns are consciously interrupted and restructured. Budgeting apps and productivity hacks may provide temporary scaffolding, but without script awareness, they cannot rewire the underlying architecture. This explains why the same person can devour financial books, download every new tool, and still find themselves in the same behavioural loops. The problem is not lack of effort. It is lack of resonance.

True behavioural transformation requires alignment at three levels: belief, identity, and system. The advice must resonate with the person's core values. It must feel congruent with the self-image they want to inhabit. And it must fit into a structure that supports rather than sabotages that identity. This is the realm of financial therapy, coaching, and reflective practices—not because they are softer, but because they are more *precise*. They work not by offering better rules, but by asking better questions. And often, those questions reveal that what looked like resistance was actually protection—an old script doing its job too well.

To make advice stick, we must reimagine it not as a prescription, but as a dialogue. Between what is financially prudent and what is psychologically resonant. Between what works on paper and what works in a human life. When that dialogue is honest, the advice no longer needs to be imposed. It becomes self-chosen. And that shift—from external compliance to internal coherence—is the difference between temporary improvement and lasting change.

Chapter 3
Mapping Your Inherited Scripts

People often confront their financial challenges by looking outward—updating a budget, switching careers, chasing a supposedly better investment. Yet the most persistent money problems rarely originate in the present. They echo across generations, transmitted silently through gesture, tone, absence, and memory. Your relationship with money was inherited long before you realised it, and seeing it clearly is the first step towards changing it.

Understanding inherited financial scripts is not about blame or nostalgia; it is about precision. Financial behaviour is rarely random. It is shaped by meaning systems—internalised beliefs, moral messages, psychological patterns—that were absorbed before you had full language or agency. These systems were adaptive once, formed from what your parents feared, revered, lacked, or survived. Because much of this influence was unspoken, it resides beneath the surface of today's decisions. What feels rational, responsible, shameful, or generous has a lineage, and that lineage can be traced.

The chapter opens with the concept of the financial genogram, a visual tool for mapping the flow of money messages across generations. This is not a family tree of names and dates; it is a diagram of influence. It captures who held money, who held power, who gave freely, who withheld in fear, who lived in scarcity despite apparent wealth. It allows us to trace not just behaviours, but meanings. A grandmother who equated spending with recklessness, echoed by a father controlling finances rigidly, can create a pattern that survives in your adult reluctance to spend—even if your earnings are ample. The genogram surfaces connections conventional financial analysis misses entirely.

To make this practical, the chapter introduces script-identification exercises—targeted prompts and pattern recognitions designed to reveal core money beliefs, many operating beneath conscious awareness. These are not casual journaling questions. They are diagnostic: What financial behaviours in others elicit judgment? What was it dangerous to want as a child? These queries aim to disrupt automaticity and illuminate what has silently shaped your financial life.

A deeper challenge lies in distinguishing symptoms from sources. Overspending, under-saving, chronic anxiety, or fear of negotiating pay are rarely root problems—they are manifestations of underlying scripts. Someone who under-earns may unconsciously believe earning more will provoke envy, disconnection, or abandonment. Another may hoard savings because their internal script dictates that safety must be preserved at all costs. Without tracing the source, people manage symptoms endlessly. This chapter offers a framework to break that cycle: is the problem behavioural, or a belief in disguise?

To illustrate, six common inherited scripts are explored. "Money equals love" transforms financial giving into a proxy for emotional connection, fostering over-gifting, under-boundaried lending, or avoidance of confrontation. "Debt is moral failure" casts borrowing as ethical stain, breeding silence or shame. "More is never enough" masquerades as ambition but often masks persistent insecurity from early experience.

These scripts are not inherently irrational. They once served adaptive purposes. A grandparent fleeing war may have adopted scarcity-driven behaviours; a parent deprived of emotional attention may have substituted material provision for affection. Scripts are strategies, logical in context—but logic decays over time. What once protected may now constrain. Mapping becomes essential when inherited scripts no longer serve the life you intend to build.

Confronting inherited scripts also means engaging with silence. In many households, money was taboo. Absence is not neutral; it conveys meaning. Children interpret avoidance as signal: money is dangerous, conflict-laden, or off-limits. These unspoken rules are harder to trace but no less influential. Adults raised in such contexts may struggle with financial transparency—not from incompetence, but because they internalised that openness is risky.

This chapter is investigative as well as theoretical. Mapping scripts sharpens key questions: Is my financial behaviour aligned with my current values or my family's survival strategies? Am I acting from present reality or inherited fears? Do I hold beliefs I never consciously chose? These are diagnostic hinges. The answers often mark the beginning of true change—not superficial budget tweaks, but a rewiring of internal permission, identity, and meaning.

Mapping requires emotional rigour. Financial life becomes a reflection of stories not authored by you. This does not mean disowning your history or vilifying your predecessors. It means embracing complexity: recognising parents as people shaped by inherited scripts, noticing when you carry their beliefs even in opposition, and seeing patterns that recur despite conscious intention. Script inheritance is recursive, layered, and paradoxical; curiosity and discernment are the only navigational tools.

The goal is not eradication of all inherited beliefs, but awareness. A consciously chosen belief is far less likely to sabotage. The problem is not that scripts exist, but that we live by them unconsciously, mistaking them for truth. By bringing unconscious patterns into awareness, you gain the capacity to make deliberate, coherent choices about your present relationship with money.

What you map, you can interrogate. What you interrogate, you can revise. The chapter provides a structured pathway with tools, language, and examples to surface long-standing influences and, perhaps for the first time, reshape them into a life consciously chosen.

The Financial Genogram

Every person arrives at adulthood with an internal map of what money means—what it permits, what it restricts, what it says about you, and what it demands of you. But few ever stop to ask where that map came from, or how its contours were drawn. The idea that money beliefs are passed down intergenerationally is not controversial. But what remains largely unexamined is how those beliefs are encoded—not as conscious rules, but as implicit narratives, shaped by family dynamics, emotional patterns, and the invisible residue of past experiences. The financial genogram is a method for charting those influences with clarity and structure. It does for money what a family tree does for ancestry: it reveals the architecture of your financial inheritance—not in assets, but in attitudes.

Genograms have long been used in fields such as psychotherapy and family systems theory to uncover relational dynamics across generations. When applied to financial beliefs, the genogram becomes a revelatory tool. It enables individuals to map not just who earned or spent the money, but how it was spoken about, who controlled it, who feared it, who equated it with love or power or shame. Most importantly, it reveals the meanings that were *transmitted* rather than taught—what children absorbed through tone, gesture, avoidance, conflict, generosity, or deprivation. These meanings rarely arrive in the form of explicit doctrine. They are absorbed before they are understood, and enacted long before they are examined.

Consider the case of a woman who grew up in a home where her father earned the income but her mother silently managed the household books. On paper, this division may seem innocuous. But through her father's dismissive tone toward budgeting and her mother's tight-lipped anxiety over expenses, the daughter internalises a split: that money is power, and that managing it is a burden. Decades later, she may struggle to feel at ease with financial planning—not because she lacks competence, but because somewhere in her emotional coding, money management is linked to subservience and stress. She has inherited not a rule, but a script. The genogram offers a way to surface and make sense of such scripts.

A proper financial genogram moves beyond names and dates. It maps economic roles (earner, spender, saver, controller), emotional valences (stressful, shameful, generous, secretive), and generational patterns (cycles of wealth creation and loss, addiction and financial chaos, inheritance and silence). It also records financial events that left a psychological imprint: bankruptcies, windfalls, job losses, divorces involving financial betrayal. These events matter not just for their practical consequences, but for the stories they generated—stories that shape descendants' instincts around risk, security, and value. For example, if a grandparent lost everything during a recession and lived frugally thereafter, that reaction may echo two generations later in a grandchild's discomfort with spending—even in times of financial abundance.

One of the most powerful aspects of a genogram is its ability to illuminate emotional legacy. Money, though often framed as a rational domain, is emotionally saturated. Many people think their discomfort around wealth or debt is uniquely personal, when in fact it is genealogical. An individual who avoids talking about money may believe they are merely private, when what they have inherited is a multigenerational silence rooted in shame or survival. The genogram enables people to see themselves not as isolated actors making odd decisions, but as inheritors of systems—often coherent, always complex.

The process of creating a financial genogram begins with inquiry, not with assumptions. It requires asking questions that may never have been posed within a family: Who controlled the money in each generation? What financial secrets were kept? How were financial roles divided along gender lines, and what messages did that convey? Was money used as a tool for connection or coercion? What major economic events marked the lives of each generation, and how did they shape belief systems? These questions are not always answerable in full—but even partial answers provide structure. What matters is not exhaustive detail, but pattern recognition.

Importantly, the genogram is not about assigning blame. It is about achieving visibility. It reveals how people adapt to the environments they were given, and how those adaptations become scripts. For instance, a parent who grew up in instability may hoard money and discourage spending not because they are selfish, but because they associate financial security with emotional safety. Their child, raised under that model, may interpret money as a moral proxy—where thrift equals virtue and indulgence equals failure. This belief may go unchallenged for years, until that child reaches a point where their values or life circumstances diverge. At that moment, the genogram becomes not just a map, but a mirror—showing which parts of a financial identity are inherited and which can be redefined.

This tool also reveals the cultural dimensions of money scripts. Financial beliefs are not formed in family vacuum—they are embedded in larger socio-economic contexts. Class background, immigration history, racial dynamics, religious teaching, and cultural mythology all infuse the meanings attached to money. A child raised in a marginalised community may develop scripts of hyper-responsibility—feeling pressure to financially rescue extended family or represent collective success. Conversely, someone raised in a wealthy but emotionally distant household may equate money with emotional substitution. The genogram helps make these cultural intersections visible. It doesn't reduce them to stereotypes, but instead traces how structural factors become personal stories.

The utility of the genogram extends beyond diagnosis. It becomes a tool for agency. Once patterns are identified, they can be consciously retained, revised, or released. A person might realise that their scarcity mindset was adaptive for a parent who grew up during wartime, but is now constraining their own ability to invest in meaningful experiences. Another might discover that their reluctance to discuss finances with a partner stems not from personal discomfort, but from observing marital conflict around money as a child. In both cases, the genogram enables a shift—from repetition to reflection, from unconscious scripting to intentional design.

One underappreciated insight that often emerges from financial genograms is that *absence is itself a form of transmission*. Many people assume they have no inherited beliefs about money because it was never discussed in their family. But silence sends signals. When parents avoid money conversations, children often learn that money is taboo, or that questions signal disrespect, or that one should not show curiosity lest they uncover conflict. These lessons shape adult behaviour just as much as overt instruction. In mapping silence, the genogram gives form to the invisible. It allows people to see not only what they were told, but what they were never permitted to ask.

Creating a financial genogram is not a one-off task. It is an evolving process of insight, refined over time as more stories emerge and as one's own financial behaviours come into sharper focus. The point is not to reach a final diagnosis, but to cultivate a sustained orientation toward pattern recognition and belief awareness. This is particularly vital for those seeking to change intergenerational patterns—whether that means building wealth, raising financially aware children, or simply achieving a more peaceful relationship with money. Without awareness of the past, new financial choices often unconsciously replicate old dynamics.

Ultimately, the genogram reveals something vital: that financial behaviours are not merely pragmatic, but profoundly psychological. They are carriers of emotion, culture, memory, and identity. By mapping those currents, we do not erase their power—we contextualise it. And from that context, we gain the clarity to choose differently. Not out of rebellion, not out of guilt, but out of understanding. The genogram does not flatten our history; it dignifies it. And in doing so, it offers us the rarest financial asset of all: perspective.

Script Identification Exercises

Long before we consciously think about money, we are absorbing meaning from it. These meanings become internalised as financial scripts—automatic, often subconscious, beliefs that shape how we earn, spend, save, or avoid money altogether. Because these scripts are rarely named or examined, they tend to operate with a stealth power: quietly governing our choices while masquerading as preferences, logic, or personality. Script identification, then, is not a cosmetic exercise in self-awareness. It is a method of intellectual and psychological excavation—one that helps us distinguish inherited beliefs from actual values, and scripts from choices. To do this well, we must go beyond mere introspection. We need a structured, precise framework for recognising the patterns we carry and tracing them back to their roots.

The task is made more complex by the fact that scripts are not formed through statements alone. They emerge from what was said, what was not said, and how it felt to grow up around money. They take shape through overheard arguments, celebratory rituals, family silences, small betrayals, and unspoken loyalties. And because they are built before we can fully question them, they can feel indistinguishable from the truth.

The first challenge of script identification is noticing the script at all. By their nature, scripts operate in the background. They are not the loud, conscious narratives we speak to others, but the quiet logic that underpins our reactions. They reveal themselves through emotional reactivity, repeated dilemmas, and contradictory financial behaviour. A person may find themselves saying they want to build savings, yet feel uncomfortable when their balance rises above a certain amount. Another might express a desire for career growth while repeatedly underpricing their services. These are not signs of laziness or incompetence; they are the echo of early messages doing their work. To decode them, we must begin not by asking what we believe, but what we repeatedly do—and how we feel while doing it.

One method for surfacing scripts is to examine financial behaviours through the lens of *emotional incongruity*. When our stated goals do not align with our repeated actions, we are often witnessing a script in conflict with intention. These moments can serve as data points: not indictments of character, but invitations to investigate. Ask: When do I feel unusually anxious or avoidant about money? When does a minor financial decision provoke an outsized reaction? What patterns—positive or problematic—do I seem to return to despite attempts to change them? And perhaps most powerfully: Whose voice do I hear in my head when I make that decision?

But scripts are not formed in a vacuum. They are nested within family systems, cultural frameworks, and emotional environments. One effective approach for identifying financial scripts involves constructing a narrative timeline of early financial exposures. This includes explicit moments—being told that "money doesn't grow on trees" or that "we don't talk about finances"—as well as implicit memories: the way your parents responded to bills, how your family treated generosity, what it meant when someone lent or borrowed money, and what financial status meant in your household. Did your family equate financial success with virtue? Was poverty linked to shame or moral failing? Were financial topics avoided altogether? Each of these moments can signal an embedded belief.

The second dimension of identification involves *repetitive patterns*. If you want to understand a script, look at your financial life as a narrative and identify which chapters keep repeating themselves. This could include recurring debt cycles, habitual overspending or underspending, panic around budgeting, or chronic under-earning. It can also show up in less obvious places: a persistent belief that money will always "work itself out," or an over-identification with frugality as moral superiority. These patterns are often unconscious re-enactments of earlier emotional dynamics. If your caregivers were inconsistent providers, you might develop a script of financial hyper-vigilance. If generosity was tied to control, you may now associate receiving help with vulnerability or weakness.

Language also reveals scripts. Pay close attention to the money-related phrases that feel instinctively true to you. Phrases like "I don't deserve that," "I have to work hard for every penny," "We're just not the kind of people who have money," or "You can't trust people once money's involved" can act as script markers. The goal is not to judge or reject these phrases immediately, but to explore their origin. Whose belief is this? Is it serving me now? What would I believe if I hadn't learned this?

In practice, script identification can benefit from structured reflection. Below are several conceptually essential exercises that readers can apply with intention and rigour:

1. The Three Financial Memories Exercise

Recall and write down three significant money-related memories from childhood or adolescence. Don't select only the traumatic or dramatic—include moments that were emotionally charged, even if they seemed mundane at the time. For each memory, ask:

- What message did I receive about money in that moment?
- How did I interpret that message at the time?
- How might that interpretation still be guiding my financial behaviours today?

2. Emotional Audit of Spending and Earning

Track your emotional state during key financial activities for two weeks—paying bills, receiving income, making a discretionary purchase, discussing money with a partner. Label your emotional responses clearly: anticipation, guilt, shame, relief, pride, avoidance. Then review the log. Where is the emotional intensity disproportionate to the financial reality? These spikes can point to internalised scripts that were never updated.

3. Script-Rooted Decision Review

Choose a recent financial decision—large or small—that you now question. Instead of focusing on the outcome, unpack the decision-making process. What assumptions were you acting on? What fear or belief was guiding your choice? What would have felt like a "risky" decision in that moment, and why?

4. Intergenerational Belief Mapping

Draw a three-generation map of your family's relationship with money. For each person (where known), note their apparent attitudes: frugal, anxious, secretive, reckless, generous, proud, burdened. What phrases or behaviours do you remember them using? What financial stories define them? Then look for through-lines. Are there recurring patterns of fear, avoidance, control, or martyrdom? These legacies often filter down in more subtle and rigid ways than we assume.

As these exercises show, script identification is not about seeking psychological pathology in every choice. It is about distinguishing between what is learned and what is lived, what is inherited and what is yours to revise. It is entirely possible to carry money beliefs that once served a protective purpose—like equating thrift with security—but which now operate as limitations. The act of recognising a script is the first step to editing it.

It is also important to resist the trap of reductionism. A financial script is not a diagnosis. You are not "bad with money" or "naturally frugal" because of some fixed personality trait. Rather, you are operating from a constellation of learned meanings—some empowering, others outdated. The work is not to eradicate all inherited influence, but to bring it into awareness and examine it on your own terms. That process of conscious authorship—of turning implicit scripts into explicit choices—is where genuine financial agency begins.

Script identification, then, is less about naming a problem and more about re-authoring a life. The questions it provokes are not only about money but about freedom. What parts of your financial life feel scripted, and which feel chosen? Where are you living someone else's story? And what might it look like to revise that story, not from rebellion or shame, but from clarity and intention? The work is not easy. But it is essential. Because until a script is named, it cannot be changed—and until it is changed, it will keep writing your story for you.

Symptom or Source?

Not all financial problems stem from ignorance, irresponsibility, or lack of tools. In fact, many persist despite intelligence, motivation, and access to information. A person with a finance degree may still compulsively avoid checking their bank account. A couple earning above the national median might repeatedly find themselves in overdraft by month's end. These are not failures of budgeting technique or fiscal willpower; they are signals. And like all persistent signals, they demand interpretation. The critical skill is learning to distinguish a *symptom*—the visible expression of financial difficulty—from a *source*—the underlying belief or emotional logic driving the behaviour. Without this discernment, we risk misdiagnosing dysfunction and applying solutions to the wrong layer of the problem.

The distinction between symptoms and sources is not just semantic—it is strategic. Treating a script-based financial pattern as if it were a simple knowledge gap is like applying an ice pack to a phantom limb: soothing, perhaps, but irrelevant to the real injury. Financial advice, no matter how rational or technically sound, cannot overwrite pre-rational beliefs. Yet the self-help and financial literacy industries routinely collapse these categories. A person who overspends is offered a budgeting app. A chronic under-earner is told to "just ask for more." A couple in financial conflict is urged to have monthly money dates. These tools can be useful—but only when they match the level at which the issue operates.

The diagnostic error begins with misreading behaviour as isolated rather than encoded. Financial habits do not emerge in a vacuum. They are expressions of mental models, emotional memories, and internalised narratives—some of which are inherited, others adaptive, and many no longer relevant to present circumstances. A behaviour becomes irrational only when stripped from the script that sustains it. For example, someone who routinely undercharges for their work may appear unambitious or disorganised. But if we examine their underlying script—perhaps a belief that "earning too much will alienate others," or "I must not outshine my family"—the behaviour begins to make sense, not as a rational market decision, but as a loyalty to internal logic. *Beliefs come first; behaviour follows.*

This is why treating financial symptoms at face value often leads to temporary or surface-level improvements. A budgeting method may curb overspending in the short term, but if the overspending is driven by a script like "money is for soothing pain" or "having nice things proves I'm not poor anymore," the unresolved source will reassert itself—often through substitution. The person may simply shift their coping to another domain, like compulsive generosity or financial enmeshment with others. The outward problem appears changed, but the internal script continues to run.

To distinguish between symptom and source requires a form of psychological and situational triangulation. One helpful lens is to observe *durability and recurrence*. If a financial problem recurs across contexts, life stages, or relationships—even when surface variables change—it is likely rooted in a script. For instance, someone who finds themselves under-earning across multiple jobs and industries is probably not encountering bad luck alone. Nor is someone who experiences anxiety when saving large sums simply unfamiliar with banking. Persistent patterns point toward deeper meanings. They suggest that the behaviour is not random, but protective—serving an unconscious function such as identity preservation, emotional soothing, or relational safety.

On the other hand, some financial struggles are better explained by *informational gaps or circumstantial pressures*. A recent graduate drowning in student loan complexity may not have a dysfunctional script—just inadequate financial education. A single parent in a housing crisis may be making high-interest borrowing decisions not from a belief that "debt is normal," but because there are no viable alternatives in the moment. These examples underscore the risk of over-pathologising financial difficulty. Not every problem is the result of poor belief hygiene. Sometimes, the issue is systemic or logistical. The task is to stay honest about context while remaining curious about patterns.

One practical test to differentiate symptom from source is to examine the emotional undertow beneath the behaviour. *Is the financial action accompanied by a disproportionate emotional charge—anxiety, guilt, secrecy, shame, defiance?* If so, it may be driven by a script. Emotional overinvestment often signals that money is standing in for something else—approval, control, safety, dignity. Conversely, when a financial issue evokes primarily confusion, frustration, or indecision, it may indicate an informational gap rather than an embedded belief.

Real-world examples clarify this distinction. Consider Maya, a 41-year-old executive who saves compulsively but feels unsafe spending even on basic comforts. Her friends describe her as "responsible" and "prudent," but she privately wrestles with a gnawing fear of financial ruin despite high income and no debt. When pressed, she recalls a childhood of volatile finances, where her parents' business failures created a script: *"Security is never real—it can disappear overnight."* Her hoarding is not about greed or ignorance; it is about survival logic that outlived its context.

Contrast this with Jared, a 28-year-old freelance designer who is repeatedly late on rent, bounces between income streams, and avoids tax filings. Initially framed as financial self-sabotage, his behaviour improves significantly after a basic intervention: hiring an accountant and using an invoicing platform that automates his payments. Jared did not have a core script that demonised money or feared stability—he was simply disorganised and lacked structure. His problem was a skill gap, not a script loop.

These contrasting portraits illustrate a core insight: *Just because a financial behaviour looks dysfunctional does not mean it is psychologically rooted. And just because a person knows what to do does not mean they can do it.* Advice only sticks when it addresses the true level of the problem.

The implications of misdiagnosis are not merely academic—they are strategic. When script-driven behaviours are treated as logistical errors, interventions often fail or backfire. The person may blame themselves more harshly, believing they lack discipline or intelligence. Shame intensifies, reinforcing the very script that created the problem. This dynamic is especially damaging in high-achieving individuals, who are socially conditioned to solve problems through effort. When effort fails to dislodge a belief-driven pattern, they may interpret it as personal deficiency rather than misapplied strategy.

On the other hand, recognising a symptom as downstream of a deeper belief allows for a different kind of solution: *one that integrates insight, not just instruction.* A person who realises they associate earning with betrayal of family may begin by questioning the loyalty that underpins their income ceiling, rather than simply forcing themselves to negotiate more. A parent who overspends on their children out of guilt may find relief not in restricting their spending, but in resolving the emotional script that equates money with apology. In both cases, the financial pattern is not "fixed" in the usual sense—it is recontextualised, its emotional weight reduced, and its logic exposed. From there, behaviour often shifts organically.

Of course, this process requires time, reflection, and in many cases, support. Financial scriptwork is not a solo journey of grit and spreadsheets—it is a process of re-seeing what has always been there. But the first step is always the same: *naming the nature of the problem accurately.* When we mistake symptoms for sources, we chase our tails. When we name the source, we begin to reclaim authorship.

The most important question, then, is not "What am I doing wrong?" but "What is this behaviour protecting?" Is it guarding an identity, soothing an old pain, or preserving a relational pattern? Once that question becomes familiar—once we learn to hear the script inside the symptom—we can begin the real work of editing. Until then, financial progress remains fragile, conditional on surface compliance. But once the true source is brought to light, even the most stubborn symptom becomes movable. Because what is seen can be revised—and what is revised no longer needs to repeat itself.

The Six Most Common Inherited Scripts

Money may be counted in spreadsheets, but its true weight often lies in the beliefs it carries—unspoken, inherited, and internalised long before a person earns their first paycheque. These beliefs are not merely ideas; they function like invisible scripts, silently directing how we earn, spend, save, give, and worry. In the absence of conscious authorship, these scripts act as psychological algorithms—often outdated, contradictory, or borrowed wholesale from previous generations. Their power lies in their invisibility. Until named, they masquerade as common sense or personality, distorting financial decision-making with uncanny consistency.

The inherited nature of financial scripts explains why two people with identical incomes can have vastly different relationships with money—one compulsively hoarding, the other overspending; one anxious, the other avoidant. These differences are not simply matters of character or circumstance. They're consequences of implicit beliefs, shaped in childhood and reinforced over decades, sometimes unconsciously spanning multiple generations. Though every script is idiosyncratic in its precise texture, a handful recur with striking frequency across class, culture, and geography—each offering a portal into the internalised beliefs that distort our financial lives.

"Money equals love"

Perhaps no script is more emotionally charged—or more relationally complex—than the belief that money is a stand-in for affection. It often arises in childhood environments where emotional warmth was offered inconsistently or conditionally, and material gifts became the primary mode of expressing care. For a child who grows up receiving praise, treats, or lavish gifts in lieu of presence or attunement, the association between money and love becomes quietly encoded. Over time, this can manifest as compulsive giving, financial co-dependency, or an inability to separate financial generosity from emotional security.

Adults shaped by this script may overextend themselves financially in relationships, feel guilt when setting boundaries, or conflate receiving money with being valued. In romantic contexts, it may produce resentment when love is not reciprocated with gifts—or confusion when affection is offered without financial exchange. *The core confusion is not behavioural but semantic: money stops being a tool and becomes a love language, often without the individual realising it.*

"Debt is moral failure"

Unlike more permissive or pragmatic attitudes toward debt, this script treats borrowing as not merely risky, but shameful. It often emerges in families that experienced poverty, bankruptcy, or generational financial instability—where debt signalled helplessness or humiliation. In these environments, paying in cash was equated with virtue, and owing money meant personal deficiency, laziness, or weakness.

While a healthy scepticism of debt can encourage responsibility, the moralisation of debt often leads to counterproductive rigidity. Individuals may refuse to take strategic financial risks (like student loans or business credit), delay essential purchases, or judge others harshly for borrowing. Worse still, they may internalise deep shame if they find themselves in debt—*not because of the numbers, but because of the perceived character flaw it reveals*. This inhibits help-seeking and can drive financial secrecy.

"More is never enough"

On the surface, this script appears motivational. It is easily celebrated in productivity-obsessed cultures, especially those that valorise self-made wealth. But its deeper logic is anchored in a fear of scarcity and emotional deprivation. Often originating in childhoods marked by unpredictability—whether economic, emotional, or both—this belief converts security into a moving target. No amount of money feels sufficient, because the goal is not merely material but existential.

This script drives compulsive accumulation: of work, income, savings, assets. But it also erodes the capacity to experience sufficiency or rest. Individuals may delay gratification indefinitely, ignore quality-of-life improvements in pursuit of net worth, or develop an identity tethered to constant expansion. *Because satisfaction is equated with complacency, they never arrive—they only pursue.* Over time, relationships suffer, and joy diminishes under the weight of endless striving.

"Money will corrupt me"

This script often has moral or spiritual origins. It is especially common among individuals raised in environments that idealised self-sacrifice, equated wealth with greed, or distrusted power. In such contexts, ambition is subtly shamed, and financial aspiration is seen as a betrayal of community, identity, or virtue.

As a result, this script can sabotage earning potential and financial confidence. Individuals may downplay success, underprice their work, or reject growth opportunities on the grounds of perceived inauthenticity. They may feel guilt when earning more than their parents did, or fear disconnection from their social group if their financial trajectory exceeds the norm. *Money becomes a contaminant rather than a resource—something that distances rather than enables.* Even when opportunities arise, self-limiting beliefs quickly neutralise them.

"I must earn my worth"

This script confuses financial productivity with self-worth. Unlike the "money equals love" belief, which is outwardly relational, this one is intensely internal. It is frequently formed in environments where praise was conditional on achievement or where rest was treated with suspicion. The child learns: *value is transactional; worth is proven through effort.* Over time, this morphs into a deeply internalised productivity mandate—work becomes the price of belonging.

Adults shaped by this belief often overwork, struggle to feel enough, and fear being seen as lazy or dispensable. Even leisure can feel guilt-ridden unless it is earned through prior exertion. Financially, this can manifest as compulsive busyness, refusal to delegate, or difficulty receiving money without "deserving" it. *The result is chronic exhaustion disguised as diligence—and financial burnout masked as commitment.*

"Talking about money is dangerous"

This belief is less about money itself than the social and emotional dynamics surrounding it. It arises in families where money conversations were taboo, explosive, or fraught with power struggles. In such contexts, money becomes an emotional tripwire—too dangerous to touch. Children internalise not just the facts about money, but the *tone* around it: secrecy, discomfort, tension.

As adults, they may avoid discussing money with partners, under-communicate about finances in professional settings, or equate financial transparency with conflict. Financial intimacy becomes difficult, even threatening. Ironically, this avoidance often *creates* the very problems it seeks to avert—misunderstandings, unmet expectations, mistrust. Without language, healthy negotiation becomes impossible. The cost is not just confusion, but isolation.

Each of these scripts functions less like a conscious philosophy and more like background operating software. They shape what we notice, how we interpret, what we pursue, and what we avoid—often automatically. What makes them powerful is not just their content but their invisibility. *To rewrite a script, one must first notice they're reading from it.*

And while these six scripts are among the most common, they are by no means exhaustive. Others—like "wealth is for other people," "poverty is noble," or "money solves everything"—also shape millions of lives. The point is not to categorise people, but to equip them. When we can name what we've inherited, we are no longer held hostage by it. We can edit, adapt, or discard what no longer serves. And in doing so, we reclaim authorship—not just of our money, but of the meaning we assign to it.

Chapter 4
Culture, Class, and Money Morality

No one steps into adulthood with a clean financial slate. Long before a first bank account is opened or a salary received, people have already internalised a framework for understanding money—shaped not merely by family, but by the wider cultural and social systems in which that family exists. Socioeconomic class, ethnicity, religion, and regional tradition do more than influence habits; they embed implicit judgements about what it means to have money, to want it, to display it, or to distance oneself from it. These judgements form a moral scaffolding around financial behaviour: every decision, from saving to spending, generosity to ambition, carries ethical as well as economic weight.

This moralisation of money often hides in plain sight, embedded in the language of respectability, success, thrift, and shame. In working-class contexts, frugality may be equated with virtue, debt with danger, and financial caution with common sense. In upper-middle-class milieus, risk-taking can signal confidence, wealth accumulation competence, and financial visibility credibility. These are not merely habits; they are scripts of legitimacy, and adherence—or deviation—produces immediate social consequences.

Consider the distinction between "spending wisely" and "wasting money." It is rarely objective. Instead, inherited norms draw the line—defining what is necessary, indulgent, shameful, or aspirational. A designer handbag may read as irresponsibility in one milieu and professional polish in another. Homeownership may suggest stability to some, entrapment to others. Even the timing of life milestones—leaving home, marrying, retiring—is laden with cultural and classed expectations, often framed as personal choice while quietly echoing group loyalties.

One of the least examined aspects of money is its role as a marker of belonging. People rarely earn or spend purely for pragmatic reasons; choices are made to remain tethered emotionally to social origins. Deviating from inherited norms—surpassing them or falling short—can feel disloyal, inauthentic, even perilous. Financial visibility may be modulated to avoid envy, rejection, or accusations of arrogance. Ambition may be quietly suppressed, self-sabotage employed to preserve modesty or alignment with upbringing. These adjustments are seldom conscious, yet they wield enormous influence.

External reinforcement compounds the effect. In families where sacrifice is valorised, wealth accumulation invites suspicion. In communities where struggle is a badge of honour, ease provokes silent resentment. In diasporic contexts, money earned abroad may be treated less as personal gain than as communal obligation—distributed through remittances, dowries, or emergency support. Here, money ceases to be private; it becomes moralised, emotionally freighted, and socially charged.

These dynamics are heightened in situations of mobility or transition. First-generation graduates, children of immigrants, and professionals moving between social strata often encounter sharply conflicting financial grammars: one voice urging saving everything, another advocating investment; one discouraging conversation about money, another demanding negotiation; one rewarding stability, another risk. The tension is emotional as well as cognitive. Rational choices can feel wrong because they violate the emotional codes inherited from upbringing—loyalty, modesty, survival.

Religious frameworks further complicate matters. Some traditions prize modesty and self-denial, rendering wealth spiritually fraught. Others interpret prosperity as divine blessing, a sign of moral diligence. These frameworks shape both self-perception and judgement of others. Financial struggle may be read as irresponsibility in one context, virtue in another; prosperity admired, envied, or disdained depending on moral outlook.

Visibility is politically charged too. In marginalised communities, flaunting wealth may invite scrutiny or accusations of betrayal. Discretion becomes a strategy; underplaying success or supporting extended kin may be adaptive rather than purely voluntary. These behaviours reflect a complex moral ecology rather than casual preference.

Crucially, these moral scripts are unevenly applied. Those from working-class or marginalised backgrounds face harsher judgement for both frugality and indulgence; middle- and upper-class individuals enjoy broader latitude, with financial choices interpreted as strategic or admirable regardless of prudence. This asymmetry demonstrates that financial morality is filtered through class, not objectivity.

Even when people consciously reject inherited values, the emotional residue persists. Guilt, anxiety, confusion—responses to money are rarely about numbers alone. They reflect violations of internalised moral codes: spending too much, earning more than a parent, saving rather than giving. Often unconscious, these residues dominate behaviour even absent material necessity.

Understanding the moral dimension of money is therefore critical. Plans that ignore identity, class, and cultural scripts often fail, offering advice without empathy. Obstacles are not only informational or behavioural—they are emotional, relational, ethical. Financial decisions are navigated through allegiances, internalised values, and inherited scripts as much as through arithmetic.

This chapter illuminates these complexities. It examines how class shapes legitimacy, culture defines admiration or shame, and morality infuses financial choice. The aim is not tidy classification but clarity. Until these forces are named, they operate unseen, driving decisions that appear irrational but are in fact deeply loyal. The goal is not replacement of one script with another, but the creation of space for conscious decision-making—so financial life aligns with chosen values rather than inherited imperatives.

What Your Class Taught You About Value

Ask a person what they believe money is *for*, and their answer may sound rational, even universal—security, freedom, opportunity. Yet those surface-level statements often mask deeper, inherited assumptions about *what makes something valuable*, *what kind of financial behaviour is admirable or shameful*, and *who gets to feel legitimate in a financial context*. These assumptions are not formed in isolation. They are deeply shaped by the socioeconomic class in which a person is raised—not merely by how much money was available, but by how that money was *perceived*, *narrated*, and *morally evaluated* within their household and peer group.

Class is not just a matter of income brackets or job titles; it is a cultural blueprint that teaches people what to aim for, what to avoid, and what counts as enough. It offers implicit instruction on ambition: how much is too much, how soon is too soon, and what kinds of aspirations will be seen as admirable versus arrogant. It teaches people what *security* looks like—whether that's a paid-off house, a steady pension, a well-funded brokerage account, or simply being debt-free at month's end. And crucially, it shapes perceptions of *financial legitimacy*: who gets to be considered responsible, deserving, self-made, or respectable.

In working-class households, for example, *stability often outranks growth*. Security is prized not because of risk-aversion in the abstract, but because the margin for error has historically been so thin. When a single unexpected expense—an appliance failure, a dental emergency, a missed shift—could destabilise an entire household, it makes sense that ambition might be viewed with ambivalence. Dreams of upward mobility may coexist with a suspicion of "getting above your station," or of inviting envy and judgment by becoming visibly successful. In such environments, reliability is more than a virtue—it is a survival mechanism. Financial caution, modest consumption, and a reluctance to "flash" money are all encoded responses to economic precarity, not evidence of personal smallness or lack of imagination.

Contrast this with upper-middle-class families, where financial safety nets—intergenerational wealth, professional networks, institutional familiarity—allow for a very different relationship to risk. Here, ambition is not only permitted but expected. There is often an implicit mandate to maximise potential, to leverage assets, to make money *work*. Within these class cultures, investment—whether in property, equities, or education—is framed as prudent strategy, not a dangerous gamble. Even failure is often depersonalised: a setback to learn from, not a mark of moral failing. And success, far from being a source of shame or social dislocation, is seen as validation—proof that one is fulfilling one's destiny.

These contrasts do not just produce different financial strategies. They produce *different definitions of what makes something valuable*. A working-class parent may teach that a "good" job is one with predictable hours and a pension. A professional-class parent may encourage entrepreneurship or prestige careers even with long hours and variable income. A working-class household may see a paid-off home as the apex of success; a more affluent one may prioritise portfolio growth over property ownership. The emotional meaning of money is not fixed—it is contextual. And class context plays an outsized role in that emotional calibration.

Importantly, these internalised values do not always match external circumstances. A person may out-earn their class of origin yet continue to act from inherited scripts—hoarding money even when they no longer need to, under-investing out of distrust of financial institutions, or rejecting opportunities that feel too far removed from their roots. Others may feel a nagging guilt or identity conflict when their professional success distances them from their family's values. These experiences are not mere psychological residue; they are evidence of *unresolved cultural tension*. When people feel chronically out of step with their financial lives—spending beyond their means, under-earning their potential, avoiding growth opportunities—it is often not because they are irrational, but because they are trying to remain *loyal* to a class-coded definition of what is "good," "realistic," or "honourable."

The legitimacy of financial decisions is also class-coded. A middle-class person using debt to fund postgraduate education is typically seen as investing in their future; a working-class person using credit to cover living costs may be labelled irresponsible. Yet the structural context—access to credit, wage stagnation, social capital—differs dramatically. What one class views as savvy positioning, another may see as reckless indulgence. These judgments are not just economic—they are *moral*. And they shape not only how people see each other, but how they see themselves.

The issue is not that one class has the "right" values and another the "wrong" ones. Rather, the issue is *invisibility*. When class-based beliefs about value go unexamined, they silently drive behaviour while masquerading as personal preference or objective truth. Someone raised to believe that ambition is self-centred may downplay their goals in the workplace, only to feel frustrated and under-recognised. Someone taught that saving is always good may hoard money even to the point of deprivation, mistaking self-denial for wisdom. Someone whose parents equated financial ease with corruption may unconsciously sabotage their success out of fear of becoming morally compromised. These behaviours are not logical, but they are *emotionally coherent* within the class-based moral frameworks in which they were learned.

This becomes particularly pronounced during class transitions. First-generation professionals, for instance, often report feeling like financial impostors—uncertain about everything from tipping etiquette to investment decisions, doubting their right to ask for raises or charge higher rates, or feeling torn between family loyalty and personal advancement. Their uncertainty is not rooted in incompetence. It is rooted in the fact that they are navigating multiple—and often contradictory—standards of value. What counts as sensible, generous, or impressive in one world may read as naïve, selfish, or showy in another. These are not trivial anxieties. They are *identity dilemmas*, triggered by a shift in class context that outpaces the internal scripts people carry.

Even financial advice is filtered through class assumptions. Budgeting strategies that work for middle-class households—like long-term investment planning or aggressive retirement saving—may feel alien or unrealistic to those who grew up paycheck to paycheck. Conversely, ideas about thrift and sacrifice from working-class cultures may be dismissed as unambitious or limiting by financial advisors who assume a background of abundance. Without script awareness, even the most practical tools become alienating, because they ask people to act against their learned instincts without understanding where those instincts came from.

Understanding what your class taught you about value is not about blaming your upbringing or discarding its lessons wholesale. It is about *contextualising your financial worldview*. It allows you to ask: which of these beliefs are still serving me? Which were adaptive in a different context, but are now outdated? Which assumptions am I unconsciously clinging to because they help me feel grounded, accepted, or "good"?

These are not surface-level questions. They go to the heart of financial self-authorship—because until we see the invisible hand of class shaping our definitions of ambition, legitimacy, and security, we are not really choosing our financial lives. We are reenacting them.

And that reenactment, while comforting in its familiarity, often comes at a cost. It can constrain people's imagination about what is possible, appropriate, or allowed. It can make certain career paths feel unthinkable, certain financial moves feel suspect, and certain forms of success feel fraudulent. It can cause people to cling to jobs they've outgrown, relationships that drain them, or financial habits that no longer make sense—because those choices preserve an internalised sense of belonging to their class of origin. What's at stake here is not just money. It is *identity, morality, and emotional safety*.

To rewrite our financial scripts in a meaningful way, we must begin by seeing the class narratives they come wrapped in. We must disentangle what is truly ours from what we inherited uncritically. Only then can we construct a values framework that reflects not just where we came from, but who we are becoming. The goal is not to "rise above" one's class or to adopt someone else's standards wholesale. The goal is *agency*—to choose one's financial beliefs consciously, rather than acting them out automatically. That choice begins with awareness. And awareness begins with asking, *Whose idea of value have I been living by?*

Cultural Norms and Financial Identity

A person raised in a conservative immigrant household in Leicester might feel compelled to wire half their salary to extended family overseas before they feel justified buying a new coat. Another, raised in a cosmopolitan enclave in central London, may be taught that any visible discomfort around money—talking too much about it or too little—is a form of social inelegance. Still another, from a working-class family in

Glasgow, might associate debt with moral failure yet view lottery wins with uncritical celebration. What ties these disparate financial attitudes together is not logic, nor individual personality, but something quieter and more powerful: inherited cultural norms.

Money is never just about money. It is encoded with meanings inherited from the environments that shaped us—our family histories, ethnic lineages, religious teachings, and the class cultures into which we were socialised. These forces do not simply inform what we think about money; they shape *how* we think about it, *who* we think we are in relation to it, and *what* we believe is safe, moral, or respectable to do with it. Financial behaviour, in this light, is not only an economic act but a cultural performance—one often so deeply rehearsed that the script is mistaken for instinct.

One of the most underappreciated forces in shaping financial identity is ethnicity. In many diasporic communities, particularly among first- and second-generation immigrants, money is rarely conceptualised as a private resource. It is seen instead as a communal asset, a form of intergenerational glue. Among East African and South Asian families, for instance, the expectation of remittances and shared support among siblings and cousins is not negotiable—it is cultural law. In such contexts, to be financially "successful" but cut off from one's obligations is not admired; it is a kind of betrayal. That same sense of duty, however, may be interpreted in majority-white British households as a lack of boundaries or an inability to stand on one's own. What is deemed generous in one tradition may be seen as co-dependent in another.

Religious beliefs add another layer of significance to financial habits. In Islamic finance, the prohibition on interest (riba) isn't a technical footnote—it reflects a theological stance against exploitation and unearned gain. In contrast, strands of American Protestant thought—especially the so-called "prosperity gospel"—explicitly frame wealth accumulation as a sign of divine favour. Even in more secular societies, religious residues persist. Catholics may speak of guilt, Jews of intergenerational survival, Buddhists of detachment from material craving. These inherited philosophies do not simply sit at the margins of financial planning—they colour the emotional tone of spending, saving, and sharing.

National identity, too, leaves its mark on money scripts. Post-war Britain, shaped by rationing and a culture of stoicism, transmitted a subtle ideal of modesty in consumption. The idea of being "flash with money" still carries faint stigma in many circles. In contrast, American financial attitudes have often celebrated visibility—flashiness, entrepreneurial hustle, conspicuous consumption—as a form of social proof. These differing expectations can shape everything from investment risk tolerance to how one speaks about money in public. A Brit who's made millions might downplay their success for fear of social friction, while a New Yorker might see the same move as strategic self-promotion. Both approaches are logical—but only within their respective cultural grammars.

This grammar is often learned early and wordlessly. Children don't need explicit lessons to absorb their family's views on money; they pick up its emotional charge through observation. If the dinner table was quiet every time a bill arrived, or if parents bickered about shopping habits, a child may unconsciously code money as dangerous or divisive. If they heard stories of heroic thrift, they may valorise sacrifice even in situations where abundance is possible. These stories, reinforced by the surrounding community, shape what feels "normal" or "reasonable"—even if those inherited definitions no longer serve the adult navigating a different financial world.

Cultural norms also shape financial risk. In collectivist cultures, security and predictability are often prioritised over entrepreneurialism. A Nigerian student in London may feel pressure to pursue a stable profession—law, medicine, engineering—not because of innate interest but because risk-taking is seen as jeopardising the family's collective future. Meanwhile, a Canadian peer raised in an individualistic framework might feel encouraged to take financial risks in service of personal fulfilment. Both are sincere expressions of cultural value—but they will produce vastly different financial paths and identities.

Where things become complicated is when individuals internalise multiple, often contradictory, money scripts. A second-generation daughter of immigrants may have grown up under the weight of familial obligation but been educated in institutions that preach independence and personal freedom. A gay man raised in a religious environment that condemned wealth as vanity may later enter professional circles where financial success is a primary form of validation. These tensions don't resolve neatly. More often, they manifest as chronic financial anxiety, shame, or ambivalence—behaviours that appear irrational until decoded through the lens of cultural inheritance.

Consider the phenomenon of financial invisibility. In some cultural traditions—particularly those shaped by histories of persecution, colonialism, or marginalisation—there is an ingrained fear of standing out financially. This can manifest in underreporting income, avoiding luxury purchases, or keeping wealth quiet even when it has been legitimately earned. For some Jewish, Chinese, or African diaspora families, this reticence is not mere modesty; it is a survival strategy passed down from generations who equated visibility with vulnerability. In modern contexts, this can lead to self-limiting behaviours, even when the external threat is no longer present. But again, these patterns make perfect sense within the logic of cultural memory.

Conversely, some individuals may overcompensate—displaying wealth not only as a personal victory but as proof of survival. This can be particularly pronounced among those whose communities have historically been denied economic legitimacy. In such cases, money becomes more than currency; it becomes narrative. To drive the car, wear the watch, live in the postcode—these are not acts of vanity but assertions of worth, demands to be seen. What appears to others as materialism may, in fact, be a coded rebuttal to cultural erasure.

The danger lies not in these inherited norms themselves but in failing to examine them. When unexamined, they masquerade as universal truths rather than culturally specific scripts. They shape who feels entitled to wealth, who feels guilt about wanting it, and who believes they must sacrifice it for the sake of belonging. Left unchecked, these unconscious frameworks can override even the most thoughtful financial plans, creating internal friction and chronic dissatisfaction.

But awareness offers leverage. When individuals begin to name the cultural stories they have inherited about money, they can start to edit them. They may realise, for instance, that their compulsive saving is less about prudence and more about ancestral scarcity. Or that their reluctance to talk about money with friends stems not from discretion but from inherited scripts about shame. Once made visible, these scripts can be evaluated, updated, or even rewritten.

In doing so, one does not betray their culture or upbringing; one honours it more fully. Cultural inheritance is not a sentence—it is a starting point. By making the implicit explicit, individuals reclaim agency over their financial identity. They move from unconscious repetition to conscious authorship. And in that shift, new possibilities open—not only for money, but for meaning.

Money as Moral Compass

It is one of the great contradictions of modern life that money, a supposedly neutral medium of exchange, is rarely treated as neutral at all. Across cultures, generations, and social strata, money functions as more than a tool—it becomes a moral barometer. People often speak of money in the language of virtue and vice. Saving is not merely prudent—it is framed as self-discipline. Spending is not merely a transaction—it is judged as indulgence or weakness. Debt can feel like sin; wealth can evoke either admiration or suspicion. These moral overlays are so deeply embedded in our personal and collective consciousness that we rarely stop to question where they come from, or whether they serve us.

The moralisation of money begins early and often imperceptibly. Consider a child raised in a household where frugality is lionised—not just as a financial habit, but as a marker of character. "We don't waste money" carries an unspoken addendum: *because we are the kind of people who are responsible, self-controlled, and decent.* The message isn't just about resource management; it's about identity. As the child grows, financial choices become more than decisions—they become tests of personal virtue. To splurge, to borrow, even to desire too much can carry an emotional charge far beyond the numbers. It is not unusual to find adults who feel shame over a vacation, guilt for buying a designer coat, or self-contempt for falling into debt—not because the actions themselves are catastrophic, but because they violate an internal moral code inherited without conscious consent.

This internalised morality is not universal; it is shaped by cultural, religious, and familial narratives. In Protestant-influenced Western cultures, for instance, there is a long history of equating frugality and industriousness with moral righteousness—a legacy of the so-called "Protestant work ethic." Within this framework, saving is not just good for your future; it is inherently virtuous. Contrast this with traditions where generosity is the highest financial ideal. In some collectivist cultures, financial sharing with extended family—even to the point of personal sacrifice—is not just encouraged;

it is morally expected. Here, hoarding money may not signify prudence but selfishness.

This divergence underscores an important point: financial morality is not absolute. It is a narrative construction, shaped by time, place, and group identity. Yet its effects are real. People regulate their financial behaviour not just in response to practical needs or economic incentives, but in an effort to conform to the moral expectations of their social world. This often leads to internal conflict. Someone raised to believe that money should not be flaunted may feel deeply uncomfortable in a high-paying job or luxury environment, even if they've worked hard to earn their success. Another person might struggle to invest or save because they associate wealth accumulation with greed or alienation from their community. These tensions are not rational; they are psychological artefacts of moral storytelling.

The moral lens can also distort how we perceive others. Society tends to admire stories of wealth "earned through hard work," but grows ambivalent—if not outright critical—of inherited wealth, lottery winnings, or speculative gains. We celebrate rags-to-riches narratives precisely because they affirm a particular moral schema: effort equals reward, virtue leads to prosperity. When money appears untethered from effort, or when it is gained through means deemed insufficiently noble, suspicion creeps in. This is why financially successful individuals often feel compelled to emphasise how hard they've worked, how long they struggled, or how much they give back. It is not enough to have money; one must also demonstrate that the money was earned in a morally acceptable fashion.

On the flip side, poverty too is moralised. Public narratives often frame the financially struggling in moral terms: irresponsible, lazy, or lacking willpower. This moral framing not only fuels stigma—it obscures structural realities. A single mother working two minimum-wage jobs without savings is often viewed through a different moral lens than a trust-fund beneficiary who spends lavishly but doesn't "need" to work. In neither case is money operating as a neutral resource. It becomes a proxy for deeper societal judgements about effort, character, and worth.

Perhaps the most insidious effect of moralising money is how it undermines self-awareness. Because financial choices are tied to questions of virtue, people often avoid honest introspection. It is easier to label a spending pattern as "bad" than to examine the underlying emotional need it serves. It is easier to justify chronic saving as "wise" than to explore whether it stems from fear, insecurity, or inherited scarcity scripts. When money becomes moral, it becomes difficult to approach financial patterns with neutrality. And without neutrality, it becomes nearly impossible to change them.

This moral entanglement also explains why financial advice often fails to stick. Telling someone to "just budget better" or "stop emotional spending" misses the point when the behaviour in question is bound to an identity narrative. If a person's sense of goodness is wrapped up in being generous, asking them to "pay themselves first" may trigger guilt or resistance. If another person associates financial risk with recklessness and familial disgrace, suggesting they start investing may feel not just risky, but morally wrong. In this context, change requires more than new knowledge—it requires the unwinding of inherited moral scripts that have quietly shaped what feels right or wrong.

This does not mean that financial morality is inherently toxic or misguided. In fact, moral codes can provide useful structure. They can discourage destructive excess, promote long-term thinking, and tether financial choices to broader values. The problem arises when these codes are unconscious, inherited rather than examined, or applied rigidly to oneself or others. When morality becomes dogma, it constrains rather than guides. When it remains invisible, it governs without consent.

To reclaim financial agency, individuals must become aware of their internal moral frameworks around money. This begins with identifying the implicit values that shape their financial decisions. Do they view wealth as freedom or as alienation? Is frugality a form of wisdom or a badge of self-denial? Is debt a tool or a failure? Such questions are not merely academic. They are the key to understanding why people make the choices they do—even when those choices appear irrational or self-defeating on the surface.

Ultimately, money is not a moral entity. It does not know whether it was earned or given, saved or spent, admired or resented. But human beings do. And the moral stories they attach to money shape not just their finances, but their self-concept, relationships, and social navigation. To disentangle morality from money is not to become amoral—it is to become discerning. It is to hold financial beliefs lightly enough to examine them, yet firmly enough to live by the ones that resonate. In a world that constantly sends mixed signals about what is financially "right," that discernment may be one of the rarest and most valuable forms of wealth.

Belonging, Shame, and Identity Scripts

In nearly every society, the need to belong is not merely psychological—it is existential. It predates money, transcends economics, and yet, paradoxically, finds one of its most complex expressions through financial behaviour. People do not only make money decisions based on need, aspiration, or arithmetic. Often, their choices are governed by a deeper, less visible imperative: to remain in alignment with the unspoken norms of their tribe. Whether "tribe" means family, community, social class, religious group, or ethnic background, the urge to avoid financial deviance is frequently about preserving belonging. And when financial actions threaten that alignment, the resulting shame is not simply emotional—it is social exile in slow motion.

The experience is rarely conscious. Few people would say outright, "I don't invest because that would make me feel different from my parents," or "I undercharge clients so my siblings won't think I've changed." But behaviour reveals the script. The child of working-class parents who earns a high income but spends in ways that mimic familial frugality may not be budgeting—he may be signalling loyalty. A first-generation university graduate who avoids discussing her salary increase at family gatherings may not be humble—she may be deflecting the risk of alienation. In these examples, money is not just about numbers. It is about group cohesion, identity preservation, and moral alignment.

These inherited scripts are powerful precisely because they are ambient rather than explicit. They are not usually taught through deliberate instruction but absorbed through atmosphere. A child might never be told, "It's shameful to have more than your siblings." But if wealth is consistently described as suspect, or if successful relatives are critiqued as "thinking they're better than us," the lesson takes root: financial advancement carries the risk of moral abandonment. Similarly, a person raised in a religious or collectivist environment might unconsciously learn that accumulating personal wealth is selfish—especially if resources are meant to be shared for the good of the whole. In both cases, the behaviour—under-earning, over-giving, or self-limiting—serves not individual goals but group continuity.

What complicates matters further is that the cost of deviation is often not monetary—it is relational. A person who earns far more than their siblings may be subtly excluded from conversations, accused of "forgetting where they came from," or quietly resented. A woman who starts investing in property while her friends struggle with debt might find herself minimising her achievements, downplaying her goals, or apologising for her ambition. This is not financial guilt in the abstract—it is shame activated by the real or perceived rupture of a belonging bond. The anxiety is not about money per se. It is about losing one's place in the circle.

Such scripts are often most potent in families where financial struggle has been a defining feature. When scarcity has been central to identity—when "we make do," "we don't have much," or "we stick together" have become cultural pillars—financial change can feel like cultural betrayal. This explains why some individuals experience success not as liberation, but as dislocation. They may find themselves torn between two selves: the one that wants to grow and the one that wants to remain recognisable. The tension isn't imagined; it is relational physics. One's shift in economic behaviour can destabilise a shared narrative, and that narrative often functions as emotional glue.

Shame plays a regulatory role in this dynamic. When someone internalises the belief that deviating from the group's financial norms makes them bad, greedy, or disloyal, they will often self-correct before conflict arises. They won't seek the promotion, won't ask for the raise, won't pursue the investment opportunity—not because they lack skill or desire, but because the anticipated shame of divergence is too costly. This is why shame is such an effective mechanism for social control: it enforces norms from within. No external enforcement is required when the group's values have been internalised to the point of self-policing.

Of course, shame is not the only outcome. Sometimes, it manifests as ambivalence, conflict avoidance, or even financial sabotage. A person might succeed in earning more money, only to spend it in ways that neutralise the gain—lavish gifts for family, unpaid debts absorbed from relatives, or business decisions made to preserve relationships rather than profits. On the surface, these may look like poor financial choices. But from an identity standpoint, they make perfect sense. They are acts of self-preservation—efforts to keep financial progress from eroding emotional belonging.

These dynamics are not confined to class or family alone. In many communities of colour, particularly in post-colonial or marginalised populations, success comes with another layer of complexity: representational pressure. An individual may feel they are not only earning for themselves but representing their community. To appear "too successful" or "too separate" can trigger accusations of assimilation, abandonment, or betrayal. Financial decisions, then, are weighed not only for personal impact but for social optics. This pressure can be exhausting. It can lead to dual-living: the private self that allows ambition and the public self that preserves familiarity.

Yet the opposite can also be true. Some groups valorise financial success as the ultimate proof of worth, perseverance, or divine favour. In these contexts, the pressure is not to minimise success, but to achieve it conspicuously—and to display it accordingly. Here, the shame lies in *not* achieving or not appearing to. One might feel compelled to spend aspirationally even when it compromises stability, just to remain in good standing with the group's success narrative. What unites these examples is that the financial script is never purely personal. It is a relational contract written in invisible ink.

To rewrite such scripts, the first step is visibility. When individuals become aware that their financial behaviours are not simply the product of personal choice but are entangled with inherited group norms, they gain the power to interrogate those norms. Not to reject them outright, but to examine whether they still serve them. Does the need to be liked by your siblings justify avoiding financial growth? Does loyalty to your upbringing require you to cap your earning potential? Is your fear of being "too different" from your friends costing you financial peace?

These questions are not easy. They cut into the heart of how people locate themselves in the social world. They challenge the false binary between financial autonomy and emotional connection. The goal is not to sever relational ties, but to create space within them for evolution. Financial growth need not equal emotional betrayal. But for that possibility to exist, group norms must be made explicit, discussed, and—if necessary—revised.

This is especially crucial in a world where economic mobility increasingly requires psychological flexibility. Those who can't examine and update their inherited money scripts often find themselves hitting invisible ceilings. They may feel inexplicably stuck, despite working hard and making strategic decisions. What they are confronting is not a technical barrier but an emotional contract: an internalised rule that says, "You can grow—but only this much, and no further."

To belong is a basic human need. But when that belonging requires self-limiting behaviours, the cost becomes too high. The challenge is to construct a new definition of loyalty—one that allows for personal financial evolution without forfeiting one's relational roots. This may involve hard conversations, temporary discomfort, or even relational renegotiation. But it also offers the possibility of fuller integration: a life where financial decisions reflect not just inherited identities but chosen ones.

The work, then, is not just financial. It is social and psychological. It is the work of untangling ourselves from inherited scripts not to reject them blindly, but to understand them fully—so that when we make a financial choice, it is ours in substance, not just in form. True financial freedom is not only the capacity to earn or save. It is the ability to belong without betraying the self, and to grow without disappearing from one's community. That balance—difficult, dynamic, and deeply human—may be the most valuable script of all.

Chapter 5
Emotional Economics

No one makes a purely financial decision. Every transfer, investment, or impulse purchase carries an emotional weight—sometimes hidden, occasionally explosive, and rarely acknowledged in standard economic theory. Classical models, with their tidy equations and rational actors, have long overlooked a more disorderly truth: money is never managed in a vacuum. We manage it from within a tangle of memory, mood, and meaning. The emotional self—fearful, proud, anxious, hopeful—often holds the controls long before the financial self opens a banking app.

What appears as budgeting, saving, or earning is frequently a form of self-regulation expressed through currency. Debt that overwhelms, cash hoarded compulsively, or gifts given beyond one's means are rarely miscalculations; they are translations of inner states into financial behaviour. Guilt masquerades as generosity. Anxiety manifests as frugality. Shame seeps into under-earning. Pride justifies unnecessary expenditure. These currents are not deviations from rationality—they are the hidden architecture of decision-making. Until they are recognised, understood, and consciously engaged, even the most rigorous financial advice remains ineffectual.

This chapter starts with a premise that may seem counterintuitive: feelings precede transactions. Emotions are not merely the result of financial outcomes—they drive them. This explains why a high earner may feel persistent insecurity, why a financially stable adult might panic at an incoming bill, or why windfalls often trigger self-sabotage. The causes lie not in spreadsheets or knowledge gaps but in emotional scripts installed early and reinforced over time—responses to perceived scarcity, threat, or inadequacy.

A common misconception in financial psychology is that money is neutral, purely instrumental. In reality, it is metaphor. Money often stands in for needs unmet through direct channels: safety, control, validation, independence. It can signify, "I am enough," "I am protected," "I am valued." These meanings, deeply personal, often remain beneath conscious awareness, subtly distorting behaviour until recognised.

Financial flashpoints—the moments that stir intense emotion—reveal these dynamics most sharply. An inheritance is rarely just an asset transfer; it becomes a referendum on loyalty and legacy. Redundancy threatens identity, not just income. Divorce settlements carry grief, shifts in power, and old scripts reactivated. In these moments, people often act compulsively or disproportionately; the emotion, not circumstance, directs behaviour.

Regression is central here. Under stress, adults often revert to early coping patterns. The financially independent professional may panic like the teenager raised in scarcity. Entrepreneurs may feel shame when charging fees, echoing early warnings against being "too greedy." This is not weakness—it is survival conditioning. When the nervous system senses threat, it activates the most familiar protection, often a financial script from a less resourced past.

Such dissonance between values and behaviour can create profound cognitive tension. Those who advocate frugality yet spend impulsively experience it keenly. Shame often compounds the cycle, eclipsing curiosity or insight. Until the underlying emotions are acknowledged, patterns persist.

Emotional economics challenges the assumption that knowledge alone drives transformation. Financial literacy, though necessary, rarely suffices. People may understand saving, budgeting, or investing, yet emotional scripts override that logic. Patterns installed through affect cannot be reasoned away—they must be felt, decoded, and consciously addressed.

Decoding does not mean abstract therapy. It requires self-awareness: noticing impulses to shop after a conflict, hesitation in opening bills, or compulsion to support unreliable relatives. Understanding that thrill-seeking in investments may be emotional, not strategic, is equally vital. Slowing decisions just enough to ask, "What am I feeling? What need is this meeting?" allows intention to align with action.

Financial and emotional boundaries are intertwined. Difficulty tolerating uncertainty, unresolved family enmeshment, or poor self-soothing skills frequently manifest as financial instability or over-extension. Recognising these connections permits interventions beyond budgets: learning to manage emotion without spending, to embrace pride without excess, to tolerate envy without shame.

Ultimately, emotional economics situates feeling at the heart of financial decision-making. Habits are reframed not as failings, but as strategies—once adaptive, now ripe for refinement. Responsibility deepens: financial empowerment is not merely prudent action; it is wise feeling. Mastery begins not with a better budget, but with insight into the emotional architecture beneath the numbers.

In the following chapters, we will explore how emotional needs intersect with money, how life events activate dormant patterns, and why relapse signals opportunity, not failure. Emotional economics is not ancillary to financial transformation—it is the transformation itself. Until money is experienced without fear, it cannot be fully mastered.

Feelings First, Money Second

Most financial decisions are not made at the cash register, inside a bank, or during a late-night spreadsheet session—they are made much earlier, in the limbic system. Long before a transaction is executed or a budget line is adjusted, the emotional brain has already registered a signal: something is wanted, feared, defended against, or avoided. Behaviour that appears irrational on the surface—such as spending beyond one's means, undercharging for professional services, or hoarding savings without purpose—often begins as an emotional reflex, not a financial strategy. Money, in many cases, is simply the visible expression of an invisible emotional state.

Traditional finance presumes rationality: people are expected to make choices based on cost-benefit analysis, long-term planning, and objective needs. But this model collapses under the weight of real-world behaviour. Consider the paradox of someone who feels acute anxiety about their financial future but simultaneously avoids reviewing their accounts. Or the person who earns well yet regularly "forgets" to invoice clients. Or the parent who overspends on their child out of guilt, then resents the resulting debt. These are not knowledge problems; they are feeling problems. *Until emotion is factored into the equation, financial behaviour will continue to elude conventional logic.*

One of the most significant drivers in this equation is fear. Fear distorts risk perception, amplifies short-term thinking, and narrows behavioural options. It pushes people into binary thinking: spend everything now or hoard compulsively; take no risks or bet everything. The person who grew up in a financially unstable household may fear scarcity so intensely that they never feel "safe" no matter how much they save. Their behaviour may look prudent from the outside—rigid budgeting, meticulous control—but inside it is governed not by rational foresight but by survival anxiety. Alternatively, a person who equates financial visibility with danger may avoid success because it would expose them to scrutiny or conflict. *Fear, in these cases, is not irrational—it is just unspoken.*

Guilt, too, is a powerful yet poorly understood financial motivator. Many people experience guilt for having more than their parents, for not helping struggling family members, or for simply desiring financial freedom when their cultural or familial norms valorise sacrifice. This guilt often manifests in compulsive giving, under-earning, or chronic underpricing. In professional contexts, it can prevent people from negotiating pay, raising rates, or even acknowledging their ambition. Guilt whispers that success is betrayal—that wanting more implies disloyalty to those who have less. The behaviour that results is often camouflaged as modesty or humility, but it is rooted in an emotional attempt to self-regulate discomfort.

Then there is pride—not the hubristic version, but the quiet emotional need for dignity, recognition, or self-validation. Pride can lead to overextending oneself financially in order to signal competence or status. It may push individuals to hide debt, refuse help, or perform a version of wealth that does not match reality. This form of emotional distortion can be particularly insidious in professional environments, where the pressure to appear "successful" may override the need for financial sustainability. The irony is that the very effort to maintain dignity can lead to instability. When pride cannot tolerate perceived weakness, it often drives people to conceal, defer, or deny necessary financial actions.

Shame, distinct from guilt, is perhaps the most paralysing of all. Where guilt says "I did something wrong," shame says "I am something wrong." It attacks identity, not action. In financial terms, shame tends to immobilise. People who carry shame around money—whether inherited from their upbringing, shaped by cultural stigma, or accrued through personal failure—often avoid financial engagement altogether. They don't open bills, don't respond to bank alerts, don't plan for the future. Not because they don't care, but because facing money means facing the self. And when the self is associated with inadequacy, failure, or fraudulence, denial becomes the only emotionally tolerable option.

These emotional triggers are not always visible in real time. They often masquerade as surface-level behaviours or "habits." But beneath the repetition lies affective data. Emotional residues from early experiences—witnessing financial conflict, being shamed for wanting, or absorbing beliefs about scarcity—become default settings. And because these patterns are emotionally encoded, they resist rational override. No budgeting app, financial planner, or spreadsheet can undo what the nervous system believes to be unsafe.

A compelling case study of this dynamic can be seen in the phenomenon of "lifestyle inflation." Conventional wisdom frames it as a simple failure of restraint: when income rises, expenses rise accordingly. But for many people, increased earning triggers deeply ambivalent emotions—especially if prosperity violates early scripts about what is acceptable or familiar. The anxiety of "becoming someone else," the fear of leaving others behind, or the discomfort of feeling visible or envied can drive compensatory spending. In this way, lifestyle inflation is not simply about consumption—it is about emotional equilibrium. *Spending becomes a way to modulate the psychological dissonance of upward mobility.*

Conversely, there are those who under-earn not out of incapacity but out of identity conflict. The individual who grew up in a household that equated wealth with greed or selfishness may unconsciously resist financial success. Their pricing remains too low, they "forget" to follow up on opportunities, or they feel uneasy when they receive too much praise or income. These are not strategic missteps—they are emotional vetoes. Success threatens to estrange them from their origin group, and so it is quietly avoided.

Even within the same financial bracket, emotional variables produce vastly different outcomes. Two individuals with the same income, savings, and debt can behave in radically different ways based on their internalised emotional narratives. One might feel resourceful and secure; the other might feel anxious and trapped. These differences cannot be explained by numbers alone. They can only be understood by tracing the emotional currents that run beneath financial life. *To change behaviour, one must first decode its emotional function.*

For this reason, effective financial change often begins not with action but with awareness. Emotional self-audit is more valuable than another spreadsheet. What emotions consistently precede your financial decisions? What physiological signals—tightness in the chest, a racing mind, numbness—appear before you click "purchase" or delay opening a bill? What patterns emerge when you examine your choices in the context of your emotional state? These questions are not indulgent—they are diagnostic. They help convert unconscious reaction into conscious response.

This work also demands a shift in how we define "financial intelligence." Too often, the concept is reduced to knowledge of investments, interest rates, or budgeting strategies. But emotional intelligence—particularly the capacity to tolerate discomfort without immediate action—is just as critical. The ability to feel envy without spending, to sit with fear without retreating, or to face guilt without appeasing is what allows for *intentional* financial behaviour. Without this capacity, one is not making choices; one is enacting emotional scripts.

The implications of this shift are profound for both individuals and professionals who work in financial contexts. Financial planners, advisors, and coaches must recognise that technical expertise is only one part of the equation. Without emotional fluency—an understanding of how affect shapes action—they risk treating symptoms while missing causes. Similarly, individuals who seek transformation must be willing to look inward as much as they look outward. Strategy without self-awareness leads to relapse; insight without emotional grounding leads to paralysis.

To put it plainly: we do not spend because we are foolish, save because we are disciplined, or invest because we are clever. We do these things because they regulate something inside us—because they soothe, compensate, validate, or protect. Until we can acknowledge this truth without shame, we remain in reaction rather than authorship. But once we recognise that every financial act is also an emotional act, a new kind of agency becomes possible—not the brittle control of repression, but the grounded clarity of integration.

Feeling, then, is not the enemy of good financial decisions. It is their foundation. The work is not to suppress emotion but to *listen to it without obeying it blindly*. To understand what each emotion wants to protect, and to ask whether there are wiser, more sustainable ways to honour that need. This is not easy work. It is slower than impulse and less glamorous than hustle. But it is the kind of work that endures—the kind that builds not only wealth, but integrity.

Emotional Substitutes for Money

Money is rarely just about money. It is often recruited—quietly, unconsciously—to perform emotional tasks it was never designed to handle. For many people, financial behaviour is less a function of numerical need than of psychological compensation. A bank account becomes a proxy for safety. A shopping spree serves as a stand-in for love. An investment portfolio becomes a source of identity. The emotional payload attached to money runs deeper than income or balance sheets; it reflects unmet needs, inherited scripts, and internalised beliefs that operate far beneath the surface of conscious choice. When emotional needs are not acknowledged directly, they find expression through financial channels—making money both a mirror and a mechanism for the inner life.

One of the most pervasive emotional substitutes people assign to money is *control*. In a world defined by uncertainty, money offers the illusion of predictability. For those who grew up in chaotic or unstable environments—where caregivers were volatile, resources were scarce, or boundaries were unreliable—financial control can feel like a lifeline. These individuals often become compulsive savers, meticulous budgeters, or financial micromanagers. The objective is not wealth creation, but *emotional regulation*. When external life feels unpredictable, the internal mandate becomes: make money obey. Budgeting apps, financial spreadsheets, and aggressive frugality become more than tools—they become talismans against disorder. *Control is not the end; it is the antidote to early helplessness.*

However, control-driven behaviour frequently spills into rigidity. The person who meticulously tracks every expenditure may experience intense anxiety over small, unplanned purchases. Generosity feels threatening, spontaneity feels unsafe, and any deviation from the financial plan can provoke disproportionate distress. What appears as "discipline" is, in fact, emotional self-defence. But the costs are substantial—relational strain, missed opportunities, and a chronic sense of tension that no amount of financial precision can resolve.

Closely related is the emotional need for *safety*. While often conflated with control, safety has a different emotional tone—it is less about mastery and more about protection. People who use money to create safety tend to view it as a barrier against vulnerability. Their financial behaviours are often motivated by fear: fear of dependence, of exposure, of future catastrophe. A large savings account is not just prudent—it is essential for psychological survival. These individuals are often unable to enjoy their resources, because doing so feels like compromising a hard-earned sense of security. They may reject risk even when it is rationally warranted, delay necessary expenditures, or underinvest in themselves and others.

The paradox here is that the pursuit of financial safety often results in emotional isolation. Because safety is interpreted through the lens of protection, intimacy feels dangerous. Offers of help are declined, financial transparency is avoided, and collaboration feels like surrender. In such cases, the boundary between self-sufficiency and emotional withdrawal becomes dangerously thin. *Safety becomes a fortress—and like all fortresses, it comes with walls.*

Money is also frequently used to fill the emotional vacuum left by a lack of *love or approval*. This dynamic often begins early, when affection or affirmation was conditional—given in exchange for achievement, conformity, or caretaking. As a result, individuals may learn to associate their worth with their ability to provide, earn, or give. Money becomes a language of validation: gifts are offered as apologies, financial support substitutes for intimacy, and success becomes a performance of worthiness. This is particularly visible in familial contexts, where parents attempt to "make up" for emotional absence through material provision, or adult children seek love from estranged parents through financial caretaking.

The difficulty with this substitution is that it distorts relational boundaries. Giving becomes entangled with needing; generosity becomes transactional. The recipient may feel burdened, the giver resentful. Moreover, because money cannot produce genuine emotional connection, the act must be repeated indefinitely. It never feels like enough—because it isn't. *Love expressed through money can create momentary closeness, but it cannot generate the kind of attunement or emotional intimacy it tries to replicate.*

Another common emotional substitution is *identity*. In a world increasingly defined by visibility and personal branding, money becomes a way to curate who we are—or who we wish to be. For some, this manifests as conspicuous consumption: designer goods, curated travel, and polished social media aesthetics. For others, it appears in more covert forms—career titles, financial milestones, or minimalist virtue-signalling. The message is consistent: *I am my financial life.* In this paradigm, money functions not as a tool, but as a mirror—reflecting value, legitimacy, and belonging.

This form of substitution is especially potent in societies where individual worth is closely tied to economic productivity. People internalise the belief that to be successful is to be valuable—and by extension, to struggle financially is to be morally deficient. Money becomes the scoreboard for selfhood. But this creates a fragile identity structure, one that is perpetually at risk of collapse. Market downturns, job loss, or unexpected expenses are no longer just financial events—they are identity threats. To lose money is to lose face; to fail financially is to disappear from view. *In this context, financial vulnerability becomes existential vulnerability.*

Importantly, these emotional substitutions are not always pathological. In moderation, they can serve adaptive functions. Saving can enhance agency, giving can express care, and financial success can foster pride. The problem arises when these behaviours become compulsive—when money is not used to serve values, but to avoid feelings. What begins as compensation becomes dependence. And over time, the person forgets the original need that money was meant to soothe.

These patterns are often reinforced by cultural and familial messages. In communities where emotional expression is discouraged, money may be the only acceptable language of feeling. A father who cannot say "I'm proud of you" might offer a cheque instead. A sibling who struggles with closeness might use birthday gifts as their only form of contact. In such cases, financial behaviour becomes the proxy for relational engagement. But the emotional content remains unspoken, and therefore, unresolved.

To unlearn these patterns, one must first develop emotional literacy—the ability to name, feel, and process core needs directly. This does not mean rejecting money, but rather reassigning it to its proper role. Instead of using money to suppress anxiety, one learns to tolerate uncertainty. Instead of offering financial support as a substitute for care, one learns to risk emotional vulnerability. Instead of chasing identity through acquisition, one begins to define the self through deeper sources of meaning—connection, contribution, integrity.

Therapeutically, the most effective interventions begin with curiosity: What need is this behaviour trying to meet? What feeling is being managed through this transaction? What am I hoping money will make me feel—safe, seen, powerful, respected? These questions interrupt the automaticity of substitution and create space for reflection. Over time, individuals can begin to experiment with more direct ways of meeting their emotional needs—ones that do not require perpetual financial performance.

The ultimate goal is not detachment from money, but *integration*. To see it not as an emotional surrogate but as a resource in service of a well-lived life. This requires maturity, honesty, and practice. But it also offers something that financial substitution never can: freedom. The freedom to use money as a tool, rather than a mask. The freedom to feel one's feelings without outsourcing them to transactions. The freedom to define value in terms that are human, not merely economic. Only then does money return to its rightful place—not as a proxy for what we lack, but as a partner in what we create.

Financial Flashpoints

Not all money moments are created equal. Some transactions—routine expenses, salary deposits, monthly budgeting—proceed with mechanical predictability, governed by habits, logic, and strategy. But others arrive with a peculiar weight, activating something older, deeper, and far more emotionally volatile. A sudden inheritance. A layoff notice. A divorce settlement. A windfall from the sale of a business. These are not merely financial events—they are *financial flashpoints*: charged episodes that disproportionately awaken inherited money scripts, buried emotional patterns, and unconscious beliefs about worth, risk, loyalty, or identity. Their volatility is not rooted in their economic significance alone, but in the psychological territory they force us to revisit.

Flashpoints are potent because they collapse time. They pull the past into the present with surprising speed, resurfacing emotions that were never consciously addressed. A grown adult receiving an inheritance may find themselves emotionally overwhelmed—not just because of the windfall, but because it symbolises a complicated parental legacy, a role reversal, or unresolved grief. Someone facing redundancy may regress not merely due to financial fear, but because it echoes early experiences of abandonment, rejection, or failure. The event *feels* bigger than it is, because it touches an emotional nerve already frayed by prior conditioning. In these moments, our financial logic is quietly overridden by psychological reflex.

Consider the case of Alex, a mid-career professional who receives a £300,000 inheritance from an estranged father. Though Alex had long imagined this moment with a sense of detachment, the actual event was disorienting. Despite his sound financial knowledge, he froze. For months, he avoided making any decisions. When he finally acted, he gave away large sums to family members and a charity his father supported—actions that aligned more with resolving unspoken guilt and performing filial duty than with any coherent financial strategy. Beneath the surface, Alex was attempting to rewrite the emotional story of their relationship through money. The inheritance was not just cash—it was *closure, apology, and reparation*. Flashpoint moments warp logic because they are saturated with meaning.

The most misunderstood flashpoints are *windfalls*. On the surface, receiving a large financial boost should feel like unambiguous good fortune. But windfalls are among the most psychologically destabilising financial events. Lottery winners, entrepreneurs who cash out, and beneficiaries of unexpected bonuses often describe feeling disoriented, guilty, or even depressed. Without a clear internal framework for integrating the new reality, they struggle to feel entitled to the gain. Old money scripts—such as "you must earn everything you get," or "rich people are greedy"—resurface and distort their relationship with the new funds. As a result, many engage in self-sabotaging behaviour: overspending, under-investing, or giving it away too quickly. What looks like irrationality is, in fact, an attempt to alleviate internal tension. *Money becomes too psychologically expensive to hold.*

Divorce, too, is a textbook flashpoint—especially when it involves a reconfiguration of financial roles. For someone who was historically the provider, divorce may trigger feelings of loss not only of the partner, but of identity and purpose. Financial negotiations in these contexts are rarely just about fair division; they are coded with narratives of punishment, revenge, resentment, and abandonment. A person might insist on "holding the line" over an asset not because they need it, but because it represents dignity, recognition, or a refusal to be erased. The spreadsheets may be rational, but the behaviour is emotional. Flashpoints distort proportionality—£10,000 may matter more than £100,000 if it carries the weight of narrative.

Layoffs or job loss also reveal the underlying architecture of one's money scripts. Those who equate earning with self-worth may experience profound shame, even when the termination was due to external factors. Others may experience panic not because of immediate cash flow issues, but because it disrupts their psychological anchors: predictability, structure, or status. The economic impact is tangible, but the emotional impact is disproportionate. These are the moments when people fall back into inherited beliefs—scrambling for any job, over-apologising to others, or withdrawing socially. It's not just about survival—it's about reclaiming an identity that suddenly feels under threat.

Financial flashpoints are not inherently negative. In fact, they often serve as powerful portals for transformation—*if* we can recognise what they are activating. The problem arises when we remain unaware of the emotional charge they carry. Because flashpoints feel urgent, people often default to fast action: moving the money, firing the advisor, launching into litigation, or making declarations like "I'll never let anyone control my money again." These reactions provide temporary relief, but often perpetuate old scripts. The wiser move is pause. Not paralysis, but thoughtful interruption. Ask: *What's really driving my discomfort? What does this situation remind me of? Whose voice do I hear in my head when I think about this decision?*

Flashpoints reveal the hidden choreography of our financial lives. They show us where autonomy ends and unconscious loyalty begins. For example, someone who grew up in a working-class family that prized modesty may feel unease after receiving a large bonus—*not* because they believe it's unearned, but because spending it visibly would violate an unspoken family rule: "Don't outshine where you came from." The discomfort is not financial—it is relational, tribal, and identity-based. Many choose to underlive their financial lives to remain emotionally aligned with their origin group. The flashpoint exposes the tension between individual agency and group belonging.

Culturally, these dynamics are compounded by societal narratives that moralise financial outcomes. Inheritances are sometimes framed as "undeserved privilege." Divorce settlements are framed as "winning" or "losing." Windfalls are framed as "too good to be true." These frames shape how people interpret their own situations. Someone receiving a large settlement after a contentious divorce may struggle to integrate it because culture has taught them to associate financial gain in divorce with moral compromise. Flashpoints become more than personal—they become social mirrors, reflecting the values, taboos, and myths of one's environment.

To navigate a financial flashpoint well requires two capacities: *self-awareness* and *emotional decoupling*. Self-awareness allows one to name what is being activated—not just financially, but psychologically. Emotional decoupling means learning to distinguish between the facts of the event and the feelings it provokes. For instance, an inheritance may be factually a gift of £500,000—but emotionally, it may feel like an unwanted torch, a burden, or a test of character. Until these feelings are disentangled, the money remains symbolically loaded and functionally paralysing.

Therapists, coaches, and financial planners often find themselves at the intersection of these flashpoints. The most effective practitioners are not those who rush into strategy, but those who hold space for the emotional undercurrents. They know that what looks like financial procrastination may, in fact, be grief. What appears to be impulsive generosity may be survivor's guilt. What sounds like an investment inquiry may be a veiled attempt to process betrayal. In this light, financial planning becomes a form of narrative reconstruction—helping individuals rewrite the story they are telling themselves about what the event means.

The value of naming flashpoints lies in their power to disrupt patterns. When we acknowledge that a financial moment is emotionally outsized, we create space for agency. Instead of acting from a place of inherited urgency, we begin to make choices that are aligned with present values. This requires slowness, reflection, and often dialogue with others who can help widen the frame. The goal is not to de-emotionalise money, but to *de-fuse* it from old narratives that no longer serve.

All of us carry dormant financial scripts—beliefs shaped by parents, culture, religion, or early experience. Most of the time, they operate in the background. But flashpoints bring them to the surface. They are not evidence of dysfunction—they are evidence of depth. They show where healing is possible, where growth is needed, and where values can be clarified. The work is not to avoid these moments, but to meet them with enough inner clarity that we do not simply replay what we inherited. In that pause—between stimulus and response—we reclaim authorship over our financial story. And that is the quiet revolution at the heart of every flashpoint: the chance to choose not just what to do with money, but *what meaning to give it.*

Why You Relapse Into Old Patterns

Stress is rarely just a physiological response; it is also a cognitive narrowing, a perceptual tightening, a reversion to what is known and previously survived. This is particularly true in the realm of money. When we experience financial uncertainty—whether through external shocks like job loss, health emergencies, or market volatility, or through internal ambiguity like career stagnation or relationship instability—we don't simply strategise; we *react.* And more often than not, we do so from earlier versions of ourselves, guided by emotional memory rather than present insight. Under pressure, we don't merely forget what we've learned—we *remember what we once relied on to feel safe.* These remembered strategies are rarely rational. They are coping scripts, inherited or self-constructed in childhood, now resurfacing like old software.

This regression is not a failure of willpower. It is an adaptive mechanism rooted in neurobiology. The human brain, when threatened, shifts from the reflective functions of the prefrontal cortex to the fast, protective reflexes of the limbic system. In practice, this means that under stress, we become more susceptible to binary thinking, more reactive to perceived loss, and more prone to interpreting financial ambiguity as danger. This biological response is adaptive in survival contexts—but in complex financial lives, it can trigger a cascade of missteps: selling too soon, overspending out of anxiety, freezing during important decisions, or enacting legacy behaviours that no longer serve.

Consider the example of Marsha, a senior executive who grew up in a household marked by financial instability. Her father's employment was erratic, and her mother responded by hoarding food and hiding cash. As an adult, Marsha became a disciplined investor and pragmatic planner—until the pandemic hit. Within weeks, she began stocking pantries, pulling money out of equities, and refusing to discuss finances with her partner. She recognised the behaviour as irrational, but felt powerless to stop it. *The crisis had activated the inner child who remembered empty cupboards and unpaid bills.* Her adult intelligence was still present, but it had been temporarily overridden by the urgency of a remembered threat.

What makes these regressions especially tricky is that they often disguise themselves as "gut instinct." The voice of a childhood coping strategy does not announce itself as such; it simply feels familiar, urgent, and compelling. For someone who grew up with a controlling parent, this might look like financial over-management—micromanaging every penny during times of stress, even when resources are secure. For someone raised in a family where emotions were avoided through retail therapy, this might look like sudden, inexplicable shopping binges during relational conflict or boredom. *The coping script is not evaluated—it is enacted.*

Crucially, financial regression is not always about doing "less mature" things. Sometimes it appears as overcorrection: becoming overly frugal, overly cautious, or perfectionistic. A man who was raised in a household where money was scarce and spending was punished may become compulsively focused on saving during economic downturns—not because the numbers demand it, but because his nervous system equates spending with danger. Even positive changes—like receiving a raise—can trigger regression if they generate identity dissonance. If deep down you believe you're "not the kind of person who earns that much," you may unconsciously sabotage the gain through poor financial choices, underpricing yourself, or overcompensating for your perceived unworthiness.

One reason regressions persist is that financial scripts are often embedded in *moral language*. We don't just believe saving is smart; we may believe it is *good*. We don't merely worry about debt; we may see it as *shameful*. These judgements are internalised early, often before we can critically examine them, and they create a powerful emotional charge around money decisions. When stressed, the part of us that fears being "bad" or "wrong" takes over, leading us to default to the rules we were given rather than the principles we have since developed. Emotional logic supersedes financial logic.

This is further complicated by the social mirroring that accompanies stress. In periods of uncertainty, people often look sideways before they look inward. They take cues from peers, family, or media—consciously or not. If one's family of origin handled money with secrecy or panic, stressful periods will reignite those scripts even if one's current environment is financially secure. The past seeps into the present not through memory, but through reflex. It's not uncommon for a person who prides themselves on their independence to find themselves making financially significant decisions that, on closer inspection, serve only to align them with familiar patterns rather than personal priorities.

Regression is also sustained by *emotional congruence*. Old patterns feel emotionally accurate under stress. They match the internal state, even if they contradict current values. If you're feeling unworthy, the action that matches that feeling—underspending on yourself, refusing to negotiate a raise, avoiding financial planning—will feel "right" in the moment. These behaviours offer emotional relief, but at the cost of long-term alignment. The problem is not that we forget what we know—it's that we temporarily mistrust it. In a state of stress, insight loses its influence, and emotional familiarity wins.

One of the more subtle drivers of regression is *identity fatigue*. Personal growth requires sustained energy: to think differently, act against instinct, challenge inherited beliefs, and live according to chosen values rather than default reflexes. During prolonged periods of uncertainty—job transitions, caregiving responsibilities, geopolitical instability—people experience cognitive and emotional depletion. In these moments, maintaining a new financial identity (e.g., "I am someone who sets boundaries," or "I make decisions based on values, not fear") becomes harder. The system reverts to energy-saving mode, and with it, familiar scripts resume. It's not failure—it's capacity triage.

Awareness is the first corrective, but it is not sufficient on its own. Simply recognising that you are regressing doesn't automatically restore clarity. What's required is *pattern interruption with compassion*. Too often, people compound regression with self-judgement: "I should know better," "I thought I was past this," "I'm just bad with money." These judgements reinforce the original scripts and deepen the cycle. What's needed is pause, not punishment. Ask: *What part of me is making this decision? What am I really trying to protect? What would I do if I felt safe right now?* These questions slow the regression and make room for choice.

Practices that reduce cognitive load—sleep, movement, reflective writing, or conversations with grounded others—can help reset the nervous system and return the mind to a more resourced state. From there, one can re-engage with financial decisions with less emotional distortion. This is not about eliminating all emotional influence (an impossible and undesirable goal), but about restoring proportionality. When your nervous system believes you're under siege, even a £50 expense can feel existential. The work is to recalibrate perception to match reality.

Importantly, regression under stress does not mean you haven't grown. It means your growth is being tested in a high-friction environment. True change is not measured by never slipping into old patterns—it's measured by how quickly and compassionately we can recover, recalibrate, and re-align. Financial maturity includes relapse. It includes self-forgiveness. It includes the humility to say, "I know better, and I also remember why this old response once kept me safe."

The antidote to regression is not discipline—it's integration. It's building a financial identity robust enough to withstand stress without splintering into outdated fragments. This requires emotional literacy: the capacity to distinguish between a real financial problem and an old emotional echo. When you can say, "This is fear, not fact," you reclaim the ability to act from the present rather than react from the past.

The question is not whether you will regress, but *how you will relate to yourself when you do*. Regression is an invitation—to revisit, re-parent, and ultimately rewrite the old script. It asks us to locate the younger part of ourselves that learned to cope through avoidance, control, or appeasement, and to remind that part: "We're safe now. We have options. We're allowed to choose differently." When this message becomes embodied, not just intellectual, the old patterns begin to lose their grip—not because they disappear, but because they are no longer the only voice in the room.

Chapter 6
Disrupting the Script

The most potent beliefs are rarely those we proclaim; they are the ones we scarcely notice. They operate silently, like unseen scaffolding beneath every choice—shaping what we spend, hoard, avoid, or fear. By the time a financial challenge presents itself, or a goal comes into view, many of us are already following a script that predates our adult reasoning and lived experience. This script, forged in childhood and tempered by culture, class, trauma, and early rewards, does not seek permission. It simply runs—until deliberate effort and insight intervene.

Disruption is not about contrarianism for its own sake. It is the conscious act of scrutinising what governs you, holding inherited beliefs up to the light, and asking: Does this belong to me? Does it serve me now? Is it true? In the realm of money—a domain dense with myths and emotion—such examination is essential. Financial scripts are enduring precisely because they masquerade as fact: "You must own a home to be secure." "Debt is immoral." "The wealthy are greedy." "Money shouldn't matter." These are not objective truths; they are interpretations, passed down through generations, reinforced by fear, by shame, rarely questioned, often obeyed unconsciously.

The difficulty lies not in their existence but in how intimately they feel like identity. When someone raised under scarcity claims, "I just can't spend on myself," they are not merely quirky—they are articulating a protective mechanism that once made emotional sense. When another insists, "I'll feel secure once I reach X savings goal," they are not laying out strategy—they are describing an emotional blueprint for safety. These are not strategies; they are stories. And stories, as any writer or psychologist will attest, are pliable if you know how to engage them.

This chapter delves into the disciplined art of disruption—not as catharsis, not as recklessness, but as structured psychological inquiry. Drawing on models such as cognitive behavioural therapy and narrative therapy, we explore how to interrogate entrenched beliefs, reframe distorted narratives, and test new mental models through deliberate action. The aim is not to purge the past entirely—such an aspiration would be both impossible and unwise—but to choose which influences remain.

Central to this work is cognitive reappraisal: actively reshaping how a belief is interpreted by tracing its origins, weighing its evidence, and evaluating its current utility. Rather than accept, "I must work hard to deserve rest," as immutable, reappraisal invites questions: Who taught me this? Under what circumstances did it arise? Does it serve me now, or is it sabotaging me? The objective is not substitution of one dogma for another, but the creation of distance, enough for the belief to become visible, examinable, and ultimately optional.

Here, the Script Audit is introduced. This is not a thought experiment; it is a structured probe into the architecture of your dominant financial belief. The audit asks you to name the script, trace its lineage, identify its emotional charge, and assess its consequences. But insight alone does not rewire behaviour. What drives change is experimentation—embodied contradiction.

Behavioural experiments are small, strategic actions that deliberately oppose your inherited script. If the belief is, "I must always save, never spend," the experiment might be a modest, non-essential purchase, held in conscious attention to discomfort. If the belief is, "Asking for more makes me greedy," the experiment may be a negotiation. These exercises are not about outcomes; they are about observing your internal response—anxiety, guilt, liberation, doubt—and using that information to guide further action.

Disruption is rarely linear. It involves friction, resistance, relapse, and gradual breakthroughs. A case study illustrates the transformation of a scarcity-dominated script into an agency-driven belief system. The story includes hesitation, setbacks, sabotage, and eventually emergence—not in a single revelatory moment, but through sustained curiosity, discomfort, and reflection.

Crucially, this work is self-restoration, not reinvention. It is not about becoming someone new but about becoming conscious of beliefs that have silently governed your financial life, and choosing—intentionally, courageously—what stays. Culture often suggests that financial transformation comes from knowledge: read more, plan better, budget harder. Knowledge is inert unless it engages the subterranean beliefs shaping how you feel about earning, spending, or managing money. This is emotional architecture, not accounting, and it demands distinct tools.

This chapter offers those tools. It provides depth to unsettle automatic responses and invite considered ones. It equips you with a language to articulate scripts with precision and a structure to revise them with integrity. It honours the origin of your beliefs without surrendering to them, treating you not as a flawed agent, but as an intelligent, adaptive individual capable of updating beliefs through insight and action.

Money is not neutral—but your relationship to it can be conscious. Scripts do not vanish; they become context rather than compass. You learn to hear the old voice without obeying it, to act from the self you are now rather than the child or culture that first shaped your sense of value. This is the promise of disruption: not erasure of the past, but the quiet, decisive refusal to be governed by it.

Cognitive Reappraisal and Rewriting Belief

Most people live inside beliefs they've never consciously chosen. These beliefs, particularly about money, are often so deeply woven into identity that questioning them feels dangerous—like betraying a parent, a class, a culture, or even oneself. "You should never owe anyone anything." "Money won't make you happy." "Talking about wealth is vulgar." These are not mere preferences or opinions. They are the architecture of a worldview—quietly shaping what feels possible, desirable, or off-limits. Yet the fact that they were inherited does not make them inevitable. Beliefs can be rewritten. Not through force of will alone, but through a methodical, psychologically grounded process of scrutiny, reappraisal, and experimentation.

Cognitive reappraisal, a concept rooted in cognitive behavioural therapy (CBT), is the process of consciously changing how we interpret a situation, thought, or memory. At its core is a simple but radical premise: *We are not the beliefs we think. We are the thinkers of those beliefs, and therefore have agency over them.* The financial implications of this idea are profound. If a person has carried the belief that "I must always save because something bad might happen," that belief likely served a purpose—perhaps offering protection in an unstable home, or signalling virtue in a scarcity-oriented culture. But when that same belief drives a 40-year-old professional to avoid investing, reject raises, or forgo enjoyment, it may be more damaging than useful. Reappraisal does not shame the belief's origin. It honours it—and then asks whether it still serves.

This questioning is not academic. It is therapeutic in the most practical sense. CBT, one of the most rigorously tested psychological interventions, teaches that thoughts drive emotions, which drive behaviour. A person who believes "I'll never be good with money" will feel ashamed, and that shame will reinforce avoidance. Reappraisal interrupts that loop. It invites the individual to identify the core belief, examine the evidence for and against it, and propose an alternative interpretation. Instead of "I'm terrible with money," the new belief might be, "I never learned good money habits, but I'm capable of developing them now." It's not positive thinking—it's truthful reframing.

But intellectual insight alone is insufficient. That's where narrative therapy extends the work. Originating in the late 20th century, narrative therapy posits that people construct their identities through stories. These stories are often inherited—family narratives, cultural myths, formative traumas—and they tend to become rigid over time. Narrative therapy invites the individual to become the *author* rather than the subject of their story. In financial terms, this might mean shifting from "I'm bad with money because my parents were" to "I come from a lineage where financial hardship was normalised, and I'm now writing a different chapter." The story remains coherent, but its tone and agency are transformed.

What makes narrative work so potent is its emphasis on *externalising* the belief. A person might name their money story—"The Responsible One," "The Scrambler," "The Invisible Earner"—and explore how that role has shaped behaviour. Once the belief is personified or externalised, it can be challenged without collapsing the self. This is particularly powerful when addressing scripts laced with shame, such as "It's greedy to want more," or "If I have money, others will expect too much." These scripts often go unchallenged because they masquerade as moral truths. Narrative therapy reveals them as interpretations—ones that can be edited, revised, or retired.

One of the most overlooked steps in rewriting belief is *locating the emotional charge*. Often, a script persists not because it is logical, but because it is emotionally anchored. For instance, someone may claim, "I'm just careful with money," but underneath lies fear—of scarcity, judgement, or loss of control. Unless that fear is addressed directly, the belief will endure regardless of rational counter-evidence. This is why cognitive reappraisal must be paired with emotional literacy. A useful question is: *What emotion do I feel when I challenge this belief? What memory, image, or warning signal does it bring up?* The more visceral the reaction, the more embedded the script. And the more it demands gentleness, not force.

The work of belief change is neither quick nor linear. One of the dangers of cognitive models is the illusion that logic can override feeling in a single stroke. In reality, beliefs change the way ice melts—gradually, from the edges. This is why small, strategic experiments are vital. A person who believes, "I must never ask for help with money," might begin by disclosing a financial challenge to a trusted friend. Someone who believes, "Spending is wasteful," might allocate £20 to an enjoyable but non-essential purchase and observe the internal reaction. These are not tests of success or failure. They are opportunities to gather evidence, observe internal resistance, and reinforce new narratives.

An essential part of the rewriting process is identifying the *utility* of the old belief. Ask not just, "Is it true?" but also, "What did this belief do for me?" A script like "Debt is shameful" may have helped someone stay frugal in college. But if it now prevents them from making a low-risk investment in their business, its usefulness has expired. Recognising the original function allows for gratitude—*this belief protected me once*—and that gratitude softens the transition to a new belief. Resentment towards old scripts only deepens inner conflict. Respectful interrogation frees the mind to evolve without backlash.

The process also benefits from context mapping. Many financial beliefs emerge from specific contexts—religious teachings, political ideologies, cultural traumas—and feel absolute because they were never positioned as local. A belief like "We don't talk about money in this family" may originate from a culture where privacy equates to dignity. Another belief—"Real success means being debt-free"—might stem from post-war generational narratives where debt was tied to collapse. Once the context is named, the belief can be held more lightly. It becomes *a truth* rather than *the truth*. That distinction makes room for alternatives.

Throughout this reappraisal process, language matters. Reframed beliefs must be crafted in language that is both aspirational and believable. Too often, well-meaning financial affirmations fall flat because they don't ring true. Replacing "I'm terrible with money" with "I'm a financial genius" creates cognitive dissonance. A more effective reframe might be, "I'm learning to make thoughtful financial choices, even when it feels unfamiliar." This phrasing honours progress without denying difficulty. It bridges the gap between shame and agency.

Finally, it is critical to name what is *not* within scope. Rewriting belief does not mean ignoring structural realities. No amount of cognitive work erases the fact that money is distributed unequally, that economic systems are biased, or that trauma impacts decision-making. But belief work *does* give people back a measure of authorship within those constraints. It helps individuals clarify what they *can* control: how they interpret their situation, how they speak to themselves about money, and how they take action from a place of intention rather than inherited fear.

In this sense, cognitive reappraisal is not a self-help technique—it is a form of psychological self-governance. It enables individuals to interrupt inherited scripts, challenge outdated assumptions, and begin to make decisions that reflect the lives they are building—not just the lives they came from. The most powerful belief you can rewrite is the one you didn't know you had. Once you see it, name it, and challenge its utility, you are no longer inside its cage. You are standing at the door, key in hand.

The Script Audit

Most people make financial decisions not based on spreadsheets or strategy, but from a place far less conscious: the money script. These are the core beliefs about money that operate like internal algorithms—quietly driving behaviour, shaping risk tolerance, dictating spending and saving habits, and colouring how one relates to wealth, work, and self-worth. A money script is not just a thought; it's a personal operating system inherited from family, culture, religion, and formative life experiences. What makes these scripts so powerful is also what makes them invisible. People don't realise they're following a script until life delivers a contradiction sharp enough to expose it.

To disrupt these patterns, we must first identify them. That is the function of the *Script Audit*—a deliberate, structured process of surfacing one dominant financial belief, interrogating its origin, and challenging its continued utility. Done thoroughly, this process does more than create insight. It creates cognitive leverage—an internal fulcrum from which lasting behavioural change becomes not only possible but sustainable.

The audit begins with one essential question: *What financial belief keeps recurring in your behaviour, even when you try to act differently?* For some, it might be the impulse to hide purchases, delay asking for a raise, or over-give in family contexts. The audit does not start with outcomes like "I overspend" or "I avoid investing." It starts with the unspoken rule behind the behaviour—*the logic you inherited, not the logic you live by.* A person might realise, for example, that they are governed by the belief: "If I ask for more, I'll seem ungrateful." That belief may not appear on any financial plan, but it shapes every negotiation, every budgeting attempt, and every relationship with money.

Once the dominant script is identified, the next step is to locate its origin. This is not a hunt for blame, but a search for context. Where did this belief come from? Was it spoken in the home—"We're not the kind of people who buy new things"? Was it absorbed through observation—a parent's anxiety when bills arrived, or a mentor's disdain for people who "flaunt" wealth? Was it culturally embedded—perhaps tied to religion, race, or region? Mapping the script's source allows the individual to see it as *acquired*, not *innate*. That shift is crucial. It invites agency.

Many people stop here—aware of the belief's origin but unsure how to challenge its grip. The audit must move into the realm of logic. What evidence supports this belief? What evidence contradicts it? Suppose someone holds the script, "I must always save, just in case." They may point to times this saved them from hardship. But what about moments where excessive saving deprived them of life-enriching experiences? The goal is not to dismiss the belief, but to test its proportions. *Is it universally true? Or contextually helpful?* Distilling when the script works and when it harms clarifies where flexibility is needed.

This stage of the audit also requires emotional honesty. Scripts are not just cognitive—they are affective. What feelings emerge when the belief is challenged? Anxiety, guilt, shame? That emotional charge reveals how entrenched the script has become. A useful exercise here is to imagine doing the opposite of the belief. If the script is "I must always be financially self-sufficient," imagine asking for help. What stories does your mind generate? "They'll think I'm weak." "I'll owe them something." "I'll lose respect." These narratives expose the emotional defences protecting the belief. The stronger the reaction, the more important it is to move forward—not away.

The final, and perhaps most underutilised, step in the Script Audit is to interrogate the *utility* of the belief. Not whether it is morally right or socially reinforced, but whether it still works for the life you are trying to build. A script may have helped a person survive a childhood of instability. But now, in adulthood, that same belief—"You can't trust anyone with your money"—may block intimacy, inhibit delegation, and undermine growth. *Every belief is a solution to a problem you may no longer have.* The audit calls this out. It separates past necessity from present limitation.

This process is best illustrated through example. Consider Ana, a 38-year-old architect from a working-class background. Her dominant script: "Security comes from not spending." Ana earned well, but lived with chronic financial anxiety. She paid cash for everything, refused to invest, and felt a surge of guilt if she spent on anything non-essential—even books or travel. Through the Script Audit, Ana traced the belief to her father, a factory worker who repeatedly said, "If you don't spend, you can't be caught short." That mantra was protective in a household with food insecurity. But Ana now had savings, stable income, and no debt. The belief no longer fit the facts.

When Ana tested the belief logically, she saw it was partially true—excessive spending *can* create vulnerability. But she also recognised how her script distorted reality. She was under-spending in areas that could enhance her well-being, relationships, and career. Emotionally, challenging the script provoked fear—she worried about "wasting" money or "becoming spoiled." Yet when Ana defined the belief's utility, she realised it had reached its expiry date. She wanted her money to serve her life, not the other way around. Ana chose a new belief: *"Security includes knowing how to use money well, not just avoid it."* That subtle reframe allowed her to begin experimenting with discretionary spending—mindfully, not impulsively.

It's worth noting that most people hold more than one money script. But in any given season of life, one script tends to dominate. The audit does not aim to cleanse all scripts at once, but to make one fully visible and reworkable. This builds confidence and skill for future audits. Moreover, the audit process respects the paradox that *many scripts are partially true but dangerously incomplete.* For example, "Money can't buy happiness" is valid in a philosophical sense—but it can buy therapy, time, and choices, all of which contribute to well-being. The audit is not interested in mantras. It is interested in function.

It's also essential to recognise the social implications of certain scripts. For people from historically marginalised communities, a script like "Don't be too visible" may protect against real discrimination. Challenging such a script must include reckoning with external realities. The audit is not an individualistic exercise detached from context. It's a tool for conscious adaptation—deciding, with eyes open, which beliefs to carry forward, which to revise, and which to retire.

Lastly, the Script Audit is not a one-time event. Like a financial review, it should be revisited periodically. As life changes—new career, relationships, parenthood, loss—the scripts that once made sense may need updating. The audit offers a repeatable framework: Identify the script. Trace its origin. Test its logic. Examine its emotional charge. Evaluate its utility. Choose what to do next. Each cycle sharpens awareness and restores authority over one's financial identity.

Done well, the Script Audit is more than introspection. It is a quiet revolution against automatic living. It brings beliefs out of shadow and into language, where they can be handled, challenged, and reshaped. And it affirms a powerful truth: *You may not have chosen your first money script, but you can choose your next.*

Behavioural Experiments

Insight without action is a well-lit cage. A person may come to understand the roots of their money script, trace its intergenerational lineage, even intellectually dispute its logic—yet still feel powerless to change. This is because beliefs are not simply cognitive artefacts; they are embodied experiences. To truly unseat a long-standing money script, one must *do* something that exposes its limitations. This is where behavioural experiments enter as a crucial, often overlooked lever of transformation. They serve as real-world stress tests for inherited beliefs—small, deliberate deviations from the script that create psychological room for a new belief to take hold.

The premise is simple: *Act as if the new belief were already true, and observe what happens.* The goal is not theatrical rebellion, nor performative risk-taking, but calibrated disruption. A behavioural experiment might involve saying "no" to a family request for money when the script says "always help," or spending £200 on a leisure activity when the script says "never waste." The experiment is not designed to achieve a financial result—it's designed to reveal an emotional truth: that the world doesn't collapse when you step outside the script. In that moment of disconfirmation, space opens for a new possibility.

Many people resist behavioural experiments because they feel artificial or scary. And that is precisely why they work. The discomfort signals that the experiment is hitting the emotional muscle of the script. Take James, a 42-year-old freelance designer raised to believe that financial security requires self-sacrifice. For years, James undercharged clients, refused help from others, and skipped holidays—believing that "good people work hard and don't indulge." In therapy, he reframed this script as outdated, rooted in his grandfather's post-war ethos. Yet insight didn't change the pattern. His therapist encouraged a behavioural experiment: *Ask for a 20% rate increase from your next client, and track your physical and emotional responses.* James did. The client agreed. But more importantly, James noticed that the anticipated guilt never materialised. He felt not indulgent, but respected. That shift didn't happen in the abstract; it happened in the doing.

The power of behavioural experiments lies in their capacity to bypass defensive reasoning. When someone tries to "talk themselves into" a new belief, the old script often counters with emotionally charged rebuttals: "You'll regret this," "They'll judge you," "This is unsafe." But when the person performs an action that contradicts the script, the brain is forced to contend with *new data.* This is why cognitive behavioural therapy (CBT) integrates behavioural experiments as a central tool: beliefs are updated most effectively when challenged by experience, not argument.

It is important, however, to structure the experiment properly. The act should be *small enough to be safe,* but *meaningful enough to evoke the script.* Too large, and the nervous system becomes overwhelmed. Too small, and the script is not truly tested. The act should also be specific and measurable. "Be more generous" is vague. "Buy lunch for a colleague without justification" is actionable. The act should be time-bound and ideally repeated. A one-off deviation may provide insight, but consistent exposure builds integration.

This framework can be applied across a range of scripts. Consider:

The scarcity script: "There's never enough." An experiment might be giving away a small sum (£20) without tracking the outcome or rationalising the gesture. What does it feel like to release money without strings?

The invisibility script: "If I have too much, I'll stand out." A person might wear a noticeable (but still authentic) piece of jewellery to a social event and observe their thoughts. Are they bracing for envy? Criticism? If nothing happens, what does that tell them?

The over-responsibility script: "I must always take care of others." One might decline a financial favour request with a kind but firm "Not this time," and sit with the aftermath—both internal and relational.

The risk-aversion script: "Money must always be safe." The experiment could be investing a nominal amount in a new venture—an amount one can afford to lose—and tracking not the financial return but the emotional journey: excitement, fear, empowerment.

What distinguishes a behavioural experiment from impulsive behaviour is *intentionality.* The act is premeditated, its purpose is learning, and the person is encouraged to journal or reflect immediately after. What emotions surfaced? Did reality match the predicted consequences? What did this reveal about the script's accuracy or exaggeration? Over time, these experiments accumulate into a body of disconfirming evidence that weakens the old belief and strengthens the neural path of the new one.

Yet there is a deeper insight here: behavioural experiments don't just test beliefs—they *rebuild identity.* When someone breaks a financial script that has governed them for decades, they are not just changing behaviour; they are changing their sense of who they are allowed to be. That is why the acts, though small, often feel seismic. A woman raised to believe that "money ruins relationships" who hires a financial planner is not just making a practical decision—she is asserting a new version of herself: one that believes she is worth clear boundaries and professional help. This identity shift is where sustainable change lives.

There is also a social dimension to these experiments. Scripts are often reinforced by community norms—what friends, families, or cultural groups silently expect. Conducting an experiment that contradicts those norms can feel like defection. A first-generation university graduate who begins to invest might be seen by family as "abandoning her roots." A person who stops covering a sibling's debts might be accused of selfishness. These reactions are not signs of failure—they are signs the experiment is working. Scripts are maintained by unspoken consensus; breaking them can unsettle the group. This, too, must be anticipated and processed.

Still, behavioural experiments are not about rebellion for its own sake. They are about agency. The goal is not to invert the old script completely, but to test its limits and refine its application. Some scripts have partial wisdom. A person who grew up poor may rightly value frugality. But a behavioural experiment might reveal where that frugality has calcified into self-denial. The script is not discarded—it is updated.

It is helpful to think of this as building a new "reference library" for the self. Each behavioural experiment becomes a page in that library—evidence of alternative outcomes, proof that new behaviours can coexist with emotional safety. Over time, these pages crowd out the old reference materials. The person no longer needs to rely on ancestral beliefs; they have a record of their own. This is how behavioural change becomes less fragile and more autonomous.

The most effective behavioural experiments are not dramatic; they are deceptively ordinary. Paying full price instead of bargain-hunting. Treating a friend without explaining. Saying "I don't want to discuss money right now" in a conflict. Each act makes a tiny incision in the narrative. Done consistently, the script begins to fray.

But perhaps the greatest value of behavioural experiments is that they place growth within reach. Insight can feel abstract. Therapy can take months. But this—this is tangible. One small act, repeated with reflection, becomes a hinge point. And that hinge, once turned, opens a door not just to new behaviour, but to a new way of being with money: less reactive, more conscious, and deeply owned.

Ultimately, behavioural experiments are not about proving the old script wrong. They are about proving the self right—the self that exists beyond inheritance, beyond fear, beyond the narratives we were too young to question. And it is in this space, one small act at a time, that financial autonomy takes root.

Case Study: From Scarcity to Agency

When people talk about money, they rarely mean money. They mean safety. Or freedom. Or shame. Or control. And more often than not, they mean history—the invisible scripts handed down through families, generations, or formative life experiences that quietly shape how they earn, spend, save, or withhold. But these scripts can be changed. Not by mere intention, and certainly not by reading advice alone, but by a lived process of reflection, resistance, and reconstruction. What follows is one such transformation. Not hypothetical. Not abstract. A real, granular journey of a woman whose financial life was governed by a deeply internalised scarcity script—and what it took for her to rewrite it.

Her name is Dana, a 39-year-old secondary school administrator from Leeds, and for most of her adult life, Dana would have described herself as "good with money." Frugal. Responsible. Never in debt. Always prepared. But beneath this confidence lived something tighter—less pragmatic and more compulsive. Dana's relationship to money was defined less by skill than by vigilance. She tracked every expense down to the pound. She avoided meals out, even with friends. She would rather patch old clothes than buy new ones. And she could not bring herself to book a holiday, not even a modest one, without a knot of guilt forming in her stomach. When she received a £5,000 performance bonus—her first in eight years—she didn't celebrate. She transferred it straight to her savings and told no one.

Dana's script, as she later articulated, was simple: *"There is never enough, and it could all disappear."* This wasn't just intellectual. It was cellular. The script had roots. Dana was raised by a single mother who worked three jobs to keep the lights on. The heating was rationed in winter, and her school lunches were quietly subsidised. Her mother taught her, not overtly but through lived modelling, that survival depended on restraint. Money was not a tool for thriving—it was a shield against collapse. Even as Dana rose professionally and was earning more than anyone in her family had before, the old template remained dominant. She lived not according to her income, but according to her inheritance—psychological, not financial.

The breakthrough did not come as a bolt of insight but as a crisis of contradiction. Dana had been offered a leadership training programme—funded entirely by her employer—that required travel and time off. She was thrilled, on the surface. But as the details emerged—a two-week residential module, some out-of-pocket expenses, and social events with high-level executives—her anxiety surged. Not just financial anxiety, but existential discomfort. The programme seemed to trigger every latent belief she held about "being too much," "spending unnecessarily," and "not belonging." She was on the verge of declining the opportunity when, in a moment of uncharacteristic clarity, she decided to book a therapy session instead.

What unfolded in therapy was the slow excavation of Dana's script. First, she gave it language. Then, she began to question its logic. Her therapist guided her through a process of cognitive reappraisal—common in cognitive behavioural and narrative therapy frameworks—inviting her to examine when this belief had originated, whose voice it echoed, and whether it remained accurate in her current life. Dana realised that while her past had demanded frugality, her present no longer required it to the same degree. Yet emotionally, she remained anchored to the past.

Insight alone, however, proved insufficient. When asked what "being freer with money" might look like in practice, Dana froze. Her body tensed. Her breath shortened. This was not just about numbers—it was about identity. To shift her script, she needed not just analysis, but action. Her therapist introduced the idea of a behavioural experiment: a small, deliberate act that would challenge her internal logic. Dana's first task was simple but seismic—to spend £50 on something she wanted, not needed, and not justify it to anyone.

She chose a massage. Not extravagant, but for Dana, it felt subversive. In the waiting room, she wanted to leave. But she stayed. During the session, she alternated between relaxation and waves of guilt. But after it ended, something shifted. She didn't feel wasteful. She felt *restored.* She wrote in her journal: *"Nothing bad happened. The world didn't end. And I actually felt more generous to others because I felt more generous to myself."*

From there, the rewiring began. Over the next three months, Dana constructed a series of micro-experiments. Buying theatre tickets without checking three discount websites first. Saying "yes" to a spontaneous dinner with friends. Allowing herself to upgrade her kitchen appliances without waiting for a sale. Each act wasn't about the money. It was about authority—her right to choose based on present values, not past fear.

Of course, there were regressions. When her boiler broke unexpectedly, Dana panicked. She found herself obsessing over repair quotes and refusing help from a friend who offered to contribute. Her therapist helped her name what was happening: *"Your old script has been activated by a financial flashpoint."* That insight softened the edge. She didn't shame herself. She took a breath. She accepted the help. And that choice marked a deeper shift: from automatic scarcity to conscious agency.

By the end of that year, Dana had not become reckless. She hadn't gone on a luxury holiday or thrown caution to the wind. But she had become *free.* She still tracked her expenses—but with curiosity, not compulsion. She still saved—but with purpose, not paranoia. And most importantly, she could now *ask herself what she wanted,* not just what she could afford. Her script had not been deleted, but it had been edited. She was no longer the frightened child policing her household budget. She was an adult with options—and with trust in her capacity to choose wisely, even with risk.

Dana's story matters not because it is dramatic, but because it is *common.* Millions live with inherited scarcity scripts that no longer reflect their financial reality. They behave as if they are still on the brink of collapse, even when the ground beneath them has stabilised. The tragedy is not overspending—it is underliving. And the path forward does not lie in spreadsheets or willpower, but in the deeper work of narrative revision.

Her journey illustrates the essential arc of transformation:

Awareness: naming the script with specificity

Interrogation: questioning its origin, logic, and relevance

Experimentation: taking small acts that reveal its limits

Integration: making choices from a place of *current truth,* not inherited fear

From scarcity to agency is not a straight line. It is cyclical, layered, and, at times, emotionally taxing. But it is also attainable. Dana didn't need to become someone else. She needed to become *more herself*—the self that had been there all along, buried beneath a script that once protected her, but now held her back.

The ultimate shift was not just financial. It was existential. Dana no longer defined success as security alone. She began to ask, "What do I value?" rather than "What do I fear?" And in that reframing lay her liberation—not from money, but from the story that had told her she didn't deserve to feel safe unless she was suffering for it.

Scarcity scripts are stubborn because they often *worked*—once. They helped people survive war, migration, divorce, instability. But when survival is no longer the primary task, these scripts can become misapplied—protecting people from a past that no longer exists, while preventing them from engaging with the richness of the present.

Agency, by contrast, is adaptive. It evolves. It doesn't deny the past but refuses to be defined by it. Dana's case, in all its nuanced detail, reminds us that money is never just about math. It is memory, meaning, and permission. And rewriting that permission may be the most powerful financial act a person can take.

Chapter 7
Relationships and Inherited Conflict

No argument about money occurs in isolation. When couples clash over a budget, siblings dispute an inheritance, or business partners reach an impasse over reinvestment, the conflict may appear to be about pounds and pence—but beneath the surface lie colliding worldviews. The friction is rarely about the cost of a holiday, the size of a gift, or a line in a spreadsheet. What is really at stake are unexamined scripts: emotional codes embedded long before the relationship began, often well before adulthood itself. Money is never merely money. It acts as a reliable proxy for fear, identity, control, trust, shame, worthiness, and legacy, giving form to what is otherwise difficult to articulate.

These inherited scripts exert a particularly powerful pull in close relationships. Individual money beliefs can feel rigid enough, but relational dynamics introduce a second, often conflicting, internal universe. Every partnership—romantic, familial, or professional—becomes a unique ecosystem of interacting scripts. What seems reasonable to one person may appear reckless to another; what feels prudent to one may signal neglect to someone else. Without a shared language and mutual recognition, even small decisions—whether where to invest, how much to spend on a meal, or whether to support a relative—can escalate into disproportionate tension.

The central insight here is that financial conflict is rarely about reason. It is about resonance. One partner's choice activates the other's internalised story. The saver who clamps down on discretionary spending may be reliving childhood scarcity; the spender resisting budgets may be reacting to a parent's obsession with deprivation. Disagreements are rarely tactical—they are emotional, historical, deeply personal. Until these layers are acknowledged and articulated, relationships remain hostage to unconscious scripts.

Take Nadia and Tom, two professionals who began living together after a year of dating. Their incomes were comparable, their values aligned around long-term planning. Yet, within three months, friction emerged over groceries, utilities, weekend outings, even petrol. Nadia wanted to pool resources; Tom insisted on tracking individual contributions. To her, separate accounts implied distance; to him, joint finances suggested control. The £40 difference in contributions was trivial compared to the emotional meanings attached. Nadia's parents had run a café and shared resources freely—love was expressed through generosity. Tom's upbringing, by contrast, emphasised autonomy; financial blending felt perilous. Until they surfaced the scripts beneath their stances, compromise felt unsafe and unsustainable.

Such dynamics are not unique to romantic relationships. Siblings negotiating parental care, adult children confronting inherited wealth, or business co-founders debating growth versus liquidity all contend with unseen script interactions. One partner may equate frugality with love; another may see generosity as duty. Risk-taking may be ambition to one and recklessness to another. Because these scripts are largely unconscious, behaviour is guided by them defensively, sometimes destructively, rather than consciously.

Inherited conflict over money tends to manifest along three axes: love, power, and control. Love is distorted when financial gestures are misread—giving mistaken for manipulation, restraint interpreted as rejection. Power distorts when income differentials are translated into decision-making authority or emotional leverage. Control distorts when historical fears—of scarcity, dependence, betrayal—shape behaviour under the guise of caution. Each axis intensifies when unacknowledged; yet, once named, these patterns can be transformed.

This chapter provides a framework for navigating such complexity with clarity and respect. We begin by unpacking the illusion of objectivity in financial conflict—what appears logical is often profoundly subjective. Next, we examine how inherited scripts around gender, class, race, and family shape assumptions about who should earn, who should spend, who decides, and what "success" looks like. These beliefs are not intrinsically flawed, but they become problematic when taken as universal truths.

A core section introduces a typology of common script pairings—recurrent dynamics observed across practice and research. Examples include The Saver versus The Spender, The Avoider versus The Tracker, and The Provider versus The Equal Partner. These pairings are not inherently problematic; friction arises when assumptions remain unnamed. By exploring how these dynamics emerge and interact, readers gain the language and insight to identify patterns in their own relationships, or those they support professionally.

Yet insight alone is insufficient. Recognition must be followed by renegotiation. The chapter presents techniques for re-scripting dialogue—communication frameworks that guide individuals from entrenched patterns toward shared understanding. These are not manipulative strategies; they are structured invitations to mutual recognition. When applied well, they allow each participant to name their script, honour its origins, and consciously decide which elements to retain or release. Dialogue thus becomes a site for co-authoring, not merely problem-solving.

The radical potential of this approach lies not in humanising money conflict—it has always needed humanising—but in treating disagreement as a doorway into intimacy, trust, and clarity. With care, money conversations can mature, rather than erode, relationships.

This chapter does not promise the elimination of tension; conflict is inevitable when differing needs intersect with finite resources. The aim is evolution: to discern when disputes are about money and when they are about meaning. To offer tools for turning inherited friction into intentional dialogue. To affirm that rewriting relational money scripts is not only possible, but essential for any partnership aspiring to equity, mutuality, and lasting growth.

When two people come together, they bring not only themselves, but also the legacies that shaped them. Only by becoming conscious authors of a shared financial narrative can they transcend the constraints of scripts they did not choose.

Money Is Never Just About Money

When two people argue about money, they are rarely just arguing about money. They are arguing about *what* money means—to them, to their past, to their safety, and to their identity. Whether the tension erupts over joint accounts, gift-giving, saving habits, or financial risk, what appears to be a rational disagreement is almost always driven by deeper, pre-conscious scripts that have little to do with arithmetic. A debate about whether to pay down a mortgage faster or invest in the market might masquerade as a technical difference, but beneath it lie emotional histories: perhaps one person associates debt with shame and the other sees delayed gratification as self-denial. The stated issue is financial. The real issue is narrative.

This principle holds true across relationships—between spouses, business partners, siblings, and even within organisations. What we often diagnose as conflict over values, ethics, or strategy is in fact a collision of internalised beliefs that have rarely, if ever, been brought into conscious awareness. In this light, money becomes not a neutral medium of exchange, but a symbol dense with psychological material. *To understand financial tension is to excavate the unspoken meanings people assign to money.*

Take, for example, the case of Priya and Alex, a couple in their late thirties who sought financial counselling after repeated fights about discretionary spending. Priya, a consultant raised by frugal immigrant parents, believed deeply in saving for emergencies and considered personal indulgences frivolous. Alex, an architect who grew up with more economic security, saw spending on leisure and travel as an affirmation of life—proof that work was not all-consuming. When Alex booked a surprise weekend away, Priya reacted with disproportionate anger—not because they couldn't afford it, but because the gesture triggered a deep, inherited anxiety about loss of control. To Alex, her response felt punitive and joyless. To Priya, it felt like survival. Both were right within their own frames. And both were unaware that what they were actually debating was *how money connects to safety and love.*

What we inherit from our families of origin are not only behaviours but emotional frameworks—scripts that encode what is acceptable, threatening, admirable, or shameful when it comes to financial life. These scripts are rarely explicit. They are absorbed through observation, repetition, reward, and consequence. A child who watches their parent panic over bills internalises the idea that money is danger. A teenager whose achievements are met with gifts may begin to equate money with love. A person whose family scorns the wealthy might come to see ambition as betrayal. Later, in adult relationships, these inherited frameworks bump up against those of others—who have their own histories, assumptions, and invisible rules.

The problem is not that people hold different money beliefs. That is inevitable. The problem is that they often *assume* their beliefs are rational, universal, and morally correct. Financial conflict then becomes moral conflict. One person sees generosity as virtue; another sees it as carelessness. One believes budgeting is discipline; the other hears it as control. The behaviour is interpreted not on its own terms, but through the lens of an inherited emotional logic.

This becomes especially fraught in high-stakes relationships. In romantic partnerships, finances often intersect with questions of power, equality, and trust. Who earns more? Who decides how it's spent? Who manages the accounts? Even in seemingly egalitarian relationships, these questions can be charged with meaning. For some, financial dependence triggers shame. For others, providing is a love language. In many cases, people are unaware of how deeply their financial behaviour is connected to gender scripts, class dynamics, or early childhood experiences of scarcity or excess.

In families, financial tension is amplified by legacy. Consider adult siblings managing the estate of a deceased parent. One may wish to distribute assets immediately; another may want to preserve property out of emotional attachment. A third might feel entitled to more due to caretaking roles. These disagreements are rarely about estate law. They are about birth order, parental approval, childhood roles, and old wounds. Money simply brings the subtext into sharp relief.

Even in professional contexts, money-related decisions are rarely free from subjective meaning. A co-founder pushing for a bold investment may be guided by a script that equates risk with courage. Their counterpart, favouring caution, may carry an inherited narrative that prudence is the highest virtue. Both argue their position on rational grounds. But behind every spreadsheet is a set of values—and behind those values, a set of emotions shaped long before the company existed.

The key insight here is not that financial conflict is emotional—that is evident to anyone who has lived through it.

The key insight is that *these emotions follow predictable, inherited patterns.* Once named, these patterns can be worked with. Left unnamed, they repeat in loops—draining relationships, distorting decisions, and reinforcing misunderstanding.

One of the most powerful shifts a person can make is to move from reaction to reflection. Instead of immediately defending a financial position, they can ask: *What is this decision protecting? What does this expenditure or restraint represent to me? Whose voice am I echoing right now—and is it still serving me?* Likewise, in conflict, rather than pathologising the other's behaviour, one can become curious: *What script are they operating from? What need is being met—or threatened—by this action?*

This is not a call for radical empathy at the expense of boundaries. There are times when financial behaviours are indeed harmful, irresponsible, or manipulative. But understanding the emotional architecture behind them does not excuse the impact; it contextualises it. And that context is often the only path to meaningful resolution.

Equally important is the realisation that *financial scripts are not fixed.* While they are often absorbed in early life, they can evolve through reflection, dialogue, and intentional experimentation. A person raised in scarcity can learn to feel safe while spending. A person raised in affluence can learn to decouple love from material proof. But none of that change is possible until the script is seen for what it is—a story, not a law.

For couples, families, and partnerships navigating financial disagreement, the goal is not to reach perfect agreement. It is to create enough mutual recognition that each person can operate from agency rather than reactivity. That might mean naming the script in play: "I realise I get tense about large purchases because my mum always panicked when the credit card bill arrived." Or it might mean naming the need beneath the behaviour: "When I want to spend on the kids, it's because I didn't have much growing up—I want them to feel abundance." These admissions shift the terrain of the conversation. They allow both parties to step out of defensiveness and into dialogue.

When money becomes symbolic—and it always does—it must be addressed symbolically as well as strategically. That is, we must engage with the emotional and narrative layers alongside the practical. A budget is not just a plan; it is a statement of priorities, values, and often, unresolved fears. A financial plan made without acknowledging these layers is unlikely to stick. It may be executed, but it will be resented—or unravelled under pressure.

The path forward, then, begins with radical honesty: not about numbers, but about meaning. That's where transformation begins—not in the ledger, but in the language we use to speak about money. In this chapter and those that follow, readers will be guided through that language—not to erase conflict, but to decode it. To see financial disagreements not as signs of failure, but as opportunities for insight. To recognise that when we fight about money, we are often fighting to protect something far older, more fragile, and more important: our sense of safety, dignity, or love.

Until we name what money means to us—and allow others to do the same—we will remain trapped in circular conflicts that masquerade as logic but are rooted in memory. Only by surfacing these meanings can we hope to build financial relationships that are not only functional, but emotionally intelligent, resilient, and free.

Love, Power, and Financial Control

It is one of the most consequential blind spots in modern relationships: while people may believe they are arguing about money, they are almost always negotiating inherited scripts about identity, security, and power. Money itself is never neutral. It is a medium through which unspoken values, psychological wounds, and generational dynamics are enacted—often with high emotional stakes. Nowhere is this more evident than in close relationships, where earning, spending, and saving cease to be mere behaviours and become moralised signifiers. What one partner views as generosity, another may perceive as recklessness; what feels like prudent saving to one may signal distrust or deprivation to another. The disagreement rarely lies in arithmetic. It lies in the emotionally loaded meanings each person has absorbed, often unconsciously, from early life.

When two people form an intimate partnership, they do not merely bring their current bank balances—they carry with them complex, often unexamined money narratives forged in the crucible of family culture. These narratives are not just beliefs about money itself, but deeply interwoven understandings of autonomy, loyalty, gender, responsibility, and self-worth. Whether one's early experience associated money with affection, control, shame, or freedom, those internalised meanings form the silent backdrop to present-day interactions. *Money becomes a language through which love and power are both expressed and contested.*

Consider the case of a couple navigating the early years of cohabitation. One partner, raised in a home where money was scarce and secrecy was the norm, may see any joint financial decision as a potential threat to autonomy. The other, whose upbringing was steeped in open dialogue and structured planning, may interpret financial opacity as evasion or mistrust. When they debate whether to merge accounts or how to allocate monthly expenses, they are not just choosing a budgeting system. They are reconciling diverging philosophies of safety and selfhood. These underlying scripts are often inherited across generations, passed down less by instruction than by observation and emotional osmosis. The parent who controlled household spending may have conveyed, without words, that financial gatekeeping is a legitimate means of establishing authority. The child who watched one parent depend financially on another may have learned that love is conditional upon economic submission. *Without conscious reflection, these early impressions calcify into default behaviours*—even in adult relationships that are otherwise egalitarian in appearance.

Power dynamics in financial relationships frequently mirror broader social hierarchies, particularly along lines of gender and generational inheritance. Although many modern partnerships endorse equality in theory, longstanding social norms still cast men as providers and women as caretakers—even when incomes suggest otherwise. These roles are rarely neutral. In heterosexual couples, for example, studies show that when women out-earn their male partners, relationship satisfaction often declines unless both parties actively interrogate and update their inherited beliefs about masculinity and financial worth. Conversely, in families where women do not earn income, the language of "helping out" or "getting an allowance" can unwittingly infantilise the non-earning partner, reinforcing scripts that equate earning with value and control with competence.

Financial dependence—whether temporary or structural—does not inevitably create imbalance. What destabilises trust is the *meaning* attached to that dependence. If one partner unconsciously associates dependence with weakness, or earning with moral superiority, then money becomes a stage for subtle and sustained contest. This dynamic is particularly visible in long-term caregiving situations, where one partner sacrifices career advancement or financial independence in service of shared goals, only to find later that the invisible labour they contributed carries less negotiating power than monetary contribution. The fallout is rarely about numbers. It is about respect, recognition, and agency.

In business partnerships and family enterprises, similar tensions play out with unique permutations. Siblings who co-manage inherited assets, for instance, may find themselves re-enacting childhood rivalries through divergent investment styles or trust structures. A controlling patriarch may maintain signature authority long after he has delegated operational leadership, signalling a deeper struggle between legacy and autonomy. Again, the surface-level dispute might involve dividends or salaries, but the emotional undercurrent is about who gets to define the future—who holds symbolic as well as practical authority.

In high-net-worth families, these tensions are often amplified. A parent who "gifts" funds while imposing conditions may believe they are acting responsibly, but recipients may experience the gesture as coercion cloaked in generosity. Conditional generosity is a hallmark of many intergenerational wealth structures—trusts, estate plans, or philanthropic foundations—that were never designed to be emotionally neutral. In such cases, financial instruments double as psychological levers. The result is a form of control that is hard to name and even harder to resist, especially when cloaked in narratives of care or duty.

It is important not to pathologise control per se. Boundaries, structure, and prudence are all legitimate and necessary elements of financial management. What distinguishes healthy financial stewardship from manipulative control is transparency, consent, and the freedom to revise shared agreements. *Coercion begins where mutuality ends.* If one partner unilaterally sets financial rules, withholds key information, or punishes dissent by limiting access, then the relationship is no longer financially collaborative—it is hierarchical in a way that undermines trust and mutual growth.

The way forward begins with curiosity. Rather than immediately challenging a partner's financial stance, it is often more effective to ask: *What belief might this behaviour be protecting?* If one person resists discretionary spending, they may not be stingy—they may fear financial collapse, having once lived through it. If another insists on elaborate gifts, they may not be wasteful—they may equate generosity with worthiness, having only received affection conditionally in childhood. These scripts are not immutable, but they are often invisible until surfaced through honest, reflective dialogue.

Shared financial planning becomes far more effective when partners articulate not just their goals, but the stories behind them. Why does one partner feel more secure with a six-month emergency fund, while the other feels anxious if too much money sits idle? Why does the phrase "my money" provoke discomfort in one and relief in another? Beneath these preferences lie fundamental assumptions about life's risks, one's role in a partnership, and the emotional uses of money itself. Surfacing these assumptions is not a one-time exercise. It is an ongoing negotiation—a process of making the implicit explicit, the invisible negotiable.

This reframing is particularly important during moments of transition: having children, losing a job, receiving an inheritance, or retiring. Such shifts often reactivate dormant scripts, which can destabilise even well-functioning partnerships. When roles change, so do expectations. A partner who was once the primary earner may struggle with diminished authority. A formerly dependent partner who steps into earning may experience guilt, resistance, or euphoria—all of which have implications for shared decision-making. *The emotional meaning of money must be revisited as often as the budget itself.*

Effective communication about money in relationships requires a delicate balance of empathy, structure, and clarity. The goal is not to eliminate difference, but to build a shared system that respects individual histories without being beholden to them. This means learning to listen for the script beneath the strategy, to validate the feeling even if the logic seems flawed. It also means developing a shared vocabulary for discussing power without blame, for exploring financial control without shaming. In mature partnerships, financial negotiation becomes a form of emotional literacy.

Ultimately, love and power need not be antagonists in financial life. When both partners (or collaborators) bring their scripts into conscious view, when they learn to translate defensiveness into dialogue, money becomes not a source of fragmentation, but a platform for shared authorship. *Control, in its healthiest form, transforms into co-creation—an intentional agreement about how two lives, or two visions, will be shaped together through financial choices.* What emerges is not just a new budget, but a new story—one in which each person sees themselves not merely as a spender or saver, an earner or dependent, but as an agent of shared financial purpose.

Script Matching and Mismatching

Some of the most persistent financial conflicts in close relationships—be they romantic, familial, or professional—are not really about money. They are about mismatched meanings. One person's sense of responsibility is another's perception of control. One's comfort with spending is seen by the other as recklessness. When these disagreements surface, they often appear as arguments over transactions, budgets, or savings rates. But underneath the surface, they are collisions between inherited financial scripts—those deeply internalised, often unconscious beliefs about what money represents, how it should be used, and what it means about who we are. Understanding the pairings and misalignments of these scripts is critical if we are to transform conflict into understanding and stagnation into growth.

At the heart of any relationship involving shared financial decisions is the convergence—or lack thereof—of internalised scripts. These are rarely explicit. Most individuals do not walk into partnerships with a clearly articulated money philosophy, let alone one that is shared with their counterpart. Instead, scripts are enacted through patterns: the automatic reaction to a credit card bill, the resistance to joint accounts, the discomfort with generosity, or the tension triggered by financial dependency. Often, we notice the pattern long before we understand its logic.

It's not difficult to imagine a classic pairing: the Saver and the Spender. The Saver was raised in an environment where financial security was paramount—perhaps shaped by economic instability, frugal role models, or chronic scarcity. Saving represents safety, foresight, and respectability. Spending, particularly on non-essentials, feels not only risky but morally questionable. By contrast, the Spender may have grown up in a household where money flowed more freely—or was used to compensate for emotional lack. To spend is to enjoy life, express care, or assert freedom. Saving, in this worldview, can feel restrictive or even punitive. Put these two scripts in a shared bank account, and you have a dynamic rife with misunderstanding. The Spender may interpret the Saver's restraint as controlling or joyless. The Saver may see the Spender's choices as impulsive or irresponsible. Neither is inherently right or wrong—each is following a script shaped by past conditions, not current realities.

Such pairings are not limited to Savers and Spenders. There is the Avoider—someone who finds money management overwhelming, confusing, or shame-inducing—matched with the Tracker, who finds comfort and competence in monitoring every pound. There is the Status Seeker, for whom financial success is a proxy for worth or visibility, partnered with the Minimalist, who sees excessive accumulation as vanity or distraction. There is the Scarcity-Driven, always anticipating financial collapse, paired with the Enough-Oriented, who is content with sufficiency and distrusts the relentless pursuit of more. Each of these combinations generates friction. Not because one person is flawed, but because their maps of reality are drawn in different ink.

Where it gets especially complex is when scripts are not only mismatched but emotionally charged. Consider the dynamic between an Overfunctioner—someone who takes excessive responsibility for the financial wellbeing of others—and an Underfunctioner, who has unconsciously come to depend on that dynamic. The former may feel pride in being the provider, yet simultaneously resentful of the pressure. The latter may feel guilty about their dependence, yet paralysed by the fear of financial autonomy. What appears on the surface as a lopsided financial arrangement is often a co-created pattern sustained by beliefs that date back to early caregiving roles, gender norms, or cultural conditioning. In these cases, financial tension is not a result of practical incompatibility but of inherited identities being unconsciously re-enacted.

The first step in navigating these mismatches is recognition. Most couples or partners do not name their financial scripts until a crisis forces the issue—debt, a major purchase, a career change, or the need to make joint decisions under pressure. At that point, the conversation can easily devolve into blame. But a more fruitful approach is to step back and ask: *What is money symbolising for each of us in this moment?* Is it freedom? Security? Approval? Control? Fear? When we ask this question, we begin to translate surface disagreements into emotional and historical terms. This is not an exercise in pop psychology; it is a necessary act of decoding.

Matching scripts can also create problems—particularly when they reinforce each other's limitations. Two Scarcity-Driven individuals may hoard money to the point of paralysis, unable to invest in meaningful opportunities. Two Spenders may encourage each other's avoidance of financial responsibility, celebrating "living in the moment" while quietly accumulating debt. In these cases, harmony can mask dysfunction. The absence of conflict does not always mean the presence of health; it may simply mean that two people are colluding in the same inherited blind spot.

A more generative possibility is found in what could be called *constructive mismatch*. When partners hold different scripts but are willing to interrogate them together, the tension can become a source of growth. The Saver can learn that not all spending is frivolous—that generosity, comfort, and joy are legitimate values. The Spender can learn that restraint is not repression but a way to honour future priorities. The Avoider can come to see that financial management is a skill, not a fixed trait. The Tracker can learn that uncertainty does not equal chaos. But for this growth to occur, there must be curiosity rather than judgement, dialogue rather than defensiveness.

This is where reflective conversation becomes essential. It is not enough to analyse our own script in isolation; we must bring it into the relational space with humility and openness. One approach is to co-create a shared financial narrative: each person names their origin script, the formative experiences behind it, and the emotional needs it still seeks to meet. This mutual witnessing can de-escalate defensiveness and create a bridge between opposing perspectives. From this place, a couple can begin to draft a *new script*—one that honours both legacies but is not limited by them.

Practically, this might mean creating systems that respect both styles: separate discretionary spending accounts to reduce micromanagement; agreed-upon thresholds for joint purchases; monthly check-ins that feel more like rituals than audits. It might also mean renegotiating the meaning of contribution. For instance, in couples where one person earns significantly more, inherited beliefs about earning power and value can quietly corrode trust. If one partner internalised the script that "earning equals authority," while the other carries a belief that "not earning equals dependency," the result is often a hierarchy that neither intended. Naming these scripts allows for a deeper conversation about worth, roles, and mutual respect.

This level of work is not only for couples. It applies equally to siblings navigating inheritance, business partners with divergent financial instincts, or even friend groups navigating shared travel plans or investment clubs. Wherever money meets relationship, scripts are at play. And wherever scripts are mismatched, there is both risk and opportunity.

What separates resilient financial relationships from brittle ones is not alignment, but self-awareness and dialogue. *The goal is not to erase difference, but to metabolise it.* When we understand our own scripts, honour their origins, and hold them lightly enough to be revised, we free ourselves from inherited reflexes. When we do the same in the presence of another, we create space for something far more robust than agreement: we build trust grounded in truth.

To navigate script mismatches, then, is to become not only financially literate, but emotionally and historically literate. It is to recognise that our responses to money are rarely just about numbers—they are about who we were told we must be, and who we are daring to become. Within this tension lies the possibility of mutual transformation, not through perfect compatibility, but through the brave act of re-writing the script together.

Re-Scripting in Dialogue

Money talk is rarely just about money. Beneath what seems like a debate over savings goals or monthly budgets often lies a much older story—one inherited, unexamined, and embedded in identity. When individuals enter financial dialogue without recognising the invisible scripts they carry from childhood, culture, or previous relationships, communication stalls and conflict deepens. Re-scripting in dialogue is not merely a communication technique—it is a disciplined process of surfacing, respecting, and revising the deeper beliefs each person brings to the table. It transforms "you never save" or "you always overspend" into a richer, more generative exchange: *what belief is being protected, what fear is being activated, and what future could be jointly rewritten?*

Every conversation about money is, in some sense, a negotiation between inherited meanings and emerging intentions. A couple arguing over whether to buy a second car may appear to be stuck on logistics, but they are often replaying scripts they absorbed decades earlier: perhaps one partner grew up in a family where financial frugality was equated with virtue, while the other saw spending as a gateway to freedom or status. Neither script is objectively correct or incorrect—but when they go unacknowledged, they harden into stances. Rescripting requires us to return to the beliefs that shaped these instincts, not to discard them indiscriminately, but to *interrogate their usefulness in a shared present.*

The starting point is personal insight. Dialogue without introspection quickly reverts to positioning. Individuals must first become fluent in their own money scripts—those persistent patterns of thought like "I must always be financially independent," "I'm not good with money," or "As long as we have enough, I don't need to worry." These beliefs often function beneath awareness until moments of relational stress expose them. Only by identifying their emotional and historical roots can they be responsibly shared—and only then can meaningful dialogue begin.

A common barrier is the assumption that financial discussions are about numbers, not narratives. But when we listen for the emotional logic behind a script, we often find an unmet need—safety, autonomy, recognition, or trust. Consider a business partnership where one founder resists hiring, citing "conservative growth." On paper, it's a risk calculus. In reality, it may stem from a parental script about self-reliance that treats delegation as weakness. Rescripting involves shifting from debate to curiosity: *Where does this resistance come from? What belief is it serving? Is it still helping us—or holding us back?*

The process of re-scripting in dialogue benefits from structured frameworks that can contain the emotional weight of these conversations. One such approach borrows from narrative therapy and nonviolent communication. Begin by naming the belief without judgement—"I grew up thinking debt was dangerous." Then contextualise it—"That was true in my parents' case; they lost their house." Then bring it into dialogue—"So when you mention financing a renovation, I don't just hear an idea. I feel fear." This kind of transparency doesn't demand agreement; it invites understanding. And in relational contexts, understanding often *precedes* agreement as the true source of resolution.

Timing and tone matter. Scripts are most rigid when individuals feel shamed, rushed, or dismissed. Re-scripting conversations must be scheduled intentionally—not layered atop logistical pressures or fuelled by reactive emotion. Creating a space where both individuals feel safe to name their beliefs without fear of ridicule is not a luxury—it is a prerequisite for adult financial intimacy. This is especially true when power dynamics are present: one partner earns more, one controls the accounts, one has inherited assets the other did not. These asymmetries cannot be erased, but they *can* be held with mutual care and maturity when both parties understand the emotional gravity of inherited beliefs.

Frameworks like the "Script-Match Dialogue" can help. Begin with mutual recognition: "We seem to have different money instincts—let's understand where they come from." Then take turns naming formative experiences: "What was the first big financial lesson you remember learning as a child?" From there, identify emotional anchors: "What does money represent to you today?" Only then move into shared visioning: "What kind of financial life do we want to build together?" By front-loading the conversation with exploration rather than decision-making, re-scripting becomes an act of co-authorship, not conflict management.

This method applies equally beyond romantic relationships. In family wealth conversations—between siblings managing an inheritance, or between adult children and ageing parents—unspoken scripts often fuel avoidance or resentment. One sibling may view inherited money as a responsibility, the other as a deserved reward. Without a shared framework to explore these narratives, even logistical choices—whether to sell a house, fund a trust, or distribute assets—become battlegrounds. Re-scripting begins by affirming that multiple truths can coexist: "You see this money as freedom; I see it as legacy. Let's find a decision that honours both."

Crucially, re-scripting in dialogue is not about agreeing on every financial choice. It is about developing a *meta-competence*—a shared ability to make meaning of differences, to hold divergent scripts without contempt, and to create new agreements that reflect evolving values rather than frozen roles. This is the hallmark of mature financial relationships: not that conflict disappears, but that it becomes a site of creativity, not reenactment.

Over time, these dialogues reshape not just individual scripts, but the collective story. Children raised in households where financial beliefs are named and discussed openly—rather than enacted through silence or blame—develop more adaptive, reflective relationships with money themselves. Teams that embed script awareness into decision-making are less likely to be hijacked by unseen agendas or unconscious sabotage. In each case, re-scripting in dialogue becomes a lever for long-term transformation.

To do this work well requires emotional stamina, linguistic care, and structural support. But the rewards are profound. When individuals feel their financial beliefs are heard, not judged—when old scripts are not pathologised, but examined—something remarkable happens. The conversation shifts from "How do we fix this disagreement?" to *"What are we really trying to protect—and what could we build if we chose differently?"* That is the work of re-scripting in dialogue: not erasing the past, but choosing the future, together.

Chapter 8
Money Scripts at Work

Most career guidance treats money as if it were an external force, a neutral tool to be mastered through strategy, timing, or skill. Yet the reality of workplace financial decisions is rarely so rational. Beneath resumes, promotions, and performance metrics lies a deeply ingrained money script: an inherited set of beliefs dictating what one is allowed to want, how much struggle is necessary, and how visible or deserving success can be. Work becomes the stage upon which these scripts perform, over and over, through salaries, contracts, and negotiated perks.

Consider the professional who hesitates to ask for a raise, weighed down by guilt. Or the founder who expands her business yet underpays herself, reinvesting every pound to defer the discomfort of personal reward. Or the consultant who overdelivers but underbills, convinced that asserting worth is manipulative. These behaviours are not random quirks—they are active scripts. Left unexamined, they become systemic: organisations reward over-workers with more work, freelancers under-earn from fear of pricing themselves out, leaders defer rest believing ease is irresponsible. The workplace, in this light, mirrors not just skill but the stories we tell ourselves about belonging, merit, and justification.

At the core of this chapter is a provocative assertion: your money script has a career. It shapes decisions, risk tolerance, visibility, and notions of "enough." It influences when you leave a role, how you advocate for yourself, how you respond to failure, and how you frame growth. Scarcity—material or emotional—can subtly link effort to worth. Witnessing instability may produce avoidance of financial power, for fear of exposure to loss. Families that prize humility may steep ambition in guilt. These inherited beliefs are not inherently flawed—they are incomplete. Ignored, they impose limits not only on income but on expression, fulfilment, and freedom.

Work magnifies these scripts because it blends identity, survival, and social validation. Unlike private spending, financial choices at work are publicly visible. This visibility invites judgment—external and internal. The professional earning far more than their parents ever did may feel disloyal; the individual turning down promotion to preserve health may feel like a failure. Such reactions are narrative, not logical, which is fortunate, because narratives can be revised.

A common manifestation is the over-working script. Cloaked in professional excellence, it stems from the belief that ease equals laziness, that worth must be earned through exhaustion. High-achieving individuals enact this script to avoid the unsettling truth that their value might be unconditional. Rest becomes threatening—not a time management problem, but a belief system issue. Addressing it requires more than boundaries; it requires re-authoring the internal story.

Its counterpart, under-earning, is often misattributed to external factors alone. While structural inequalities matter, personal money scripts are pivotal. Under-earners may carry beliefs like "I should be grateful just to be here," or "If I ask for more, I risk losing everything." These distort decisions: the consultant who avoids renegotiation, the artist who rejects lucrative opportunities fearing corruption of integrity, the academic who accepts unpaid tasks for intellectual purity. In each case, action is dictated by a script that no longer fits current capacities or values.

Entrepreneurs face similar patterns. Autonomy amplifies inherited scripts: scarcity-minded founders may overhire prematurely, fearing windows of opportunity; others hoard cash, avoiding investment due to past loss. Business models can prioritise control over scalability, not from strategy but inherited caution. Rapid expansion may replicate the hustle cultures one hoped to escape. Until awareness reaches the boardroom, legacy thinking steers outcomes.

The solution is alignment, not retreat. Script-conscious earning disentangles financial aspiration from unconscious loyalty. It asks: "What am I afraid will happen if I earn more than I am accustomed to?" Success becomes an exercise in congruence, not a justification of identity. Are earnings reflecting values, or merely replaying old patterns in more prestigious packaging?

Rewriting one's script at work follows three movements: identification, interruption, and innovation. First, recognise the core belief—not simply "I don't like negotiating," but "I believe asking for more is greedy." Second, interrupt the script by experimenting: quote higher rates, decline a flattering yet taxing role. Finally, innovate by constructing narratives grounded in chosen alignment, not inherited fear. Resistance will arise; the process is iterative. Over time, the script loosens, opening new possibilities—not because of external permission, but because internal restriction was challenged.

Throughout this chapter, we explore individuals and organisations undertaking this work: high-performing professionals unraveling over-working patterns, first-generation entrepreneurs confronting visibility fears, and teams redesigning business models to reflect abundance rather than scarcity. These are not inspirational tales; they are exercises in insight. Work becomes more than a place to earn—it becomes a laboratory where belief is enacted and can be rewritten. For those ready to undertake that work, clarity, courage, and rigour are essential companions.

Your Financial Script Shows Up in Your Career

Few people realise how much of their professional behaviour is choreographed by beliefs they absorbed long before entering the workforce. The stories we inherit—about what we're allowed to ask for, how visible we're permitted to be, and what level of ease or success we're "supposed" to enjoy—don't disappear when we step into the office, the boardroom, or the studio. They follow us. They shape how we price our work, negotiate contracts, pursue promotions, or respond to risk. *Your financial script, whether named or not, is always in the room when you make a career decision.* The only question is whether you are working for it—or it is working for you.

Take, for instance, the competent professional who consistently undercharges for her services, despite glowing testimonials and a full client roster. She tells herself it's about staying competitive, but deeper reflection reveals a familiar fear: *If I ask for more, they'll realise I'm not really worth it.* This is not about market dynamics. It is a legacy belief about worthiness, cloaked in the language of caution. In another case, a senior executive hesitates to leave a role that has long ceased to align with his values. The official reason is stability. But privately, he admits, *"I still don't feel like I've proven myself."* Here, the career stall is not due to a lack of opportunity but a script that equates loyalty to struggle with legitimacy.

Scripts around deservingness are among the most powerful and invisible forces in professional life. They determine whether we put ourselves forward or hold back. For some, these beliefs arise from growing up in environments where financial reward was associated with guilt or scarcity—perhaps there was enough, but not without tension. Others may have watched caregivers sacrifice personal wellbeing in service of financial provision, internalising the idea that fulfilment and financial stability are mutually exclusive. In adulthood, these beliefs manifest in an inability to enjoy success without anxiety, or a compulsion to overdeliver long after expectations have been met. Even when the external circumstances evolve—higher pay, better titles, wider recognition—the internal metrics remain stuck. *If we haven't re-authored the script, no promotion will feel safe enough to rewrite it.*

Visibility, too, is often governed by unspoken beliefs. Some professionals thrive on stage, others shrink from it—not because they lack skill, but because they associate being seen with danger. Visibility scripts tend to originate in environments where standing out brought criticism, envy, or rejection. In adult life, this might show up as reluctance to claim credit, avoidance of public speaking, or chronic deferral to others in decision-making spaces. It can also take subtler forms: choosing job roles that allow one to contribute without taking the spotlight, or hesitating to publish or market one's own ideas. This is not modesty—it is self-protection. And yet in today's knowledge economy, where thought leadership, personal branding, and advocacy are increasingly linked to opportunity, the cost of invisibility is often career stagnation.

Risk scripts exert equally potent influence. Some people are disproportionately risk-averse, others risk-seeking, but few have examined why. A belief like *"security must come before fulfilment"* may lead someone to stay in a job long past its expiration date, rationalising that they're being "responsible." Another person, raised in a volatile financial environment, may have developed a compensatory relationship to risk—leaping from one venture to the next in an effort to stay ahead of potential loss. Neither pattern is inherently wrong. But when risk-taking is governed by fear—or fear disguised as prudence—it becomes reactive, not strategic. The key distinction is whether the action is consciously chosen or automatically repeated. *Script-driven behaviour often masquerades as pragmatism, but beneath the surface is a rehearsed survival mechanism.*

Entrepreneurs offer a particularly vivid case study. The myth of the self-made founder often obscures the fact that businesses, like people, reflect inherited beliefs. A founder who grew up in a household where money was scarce but effort was endless may unconsciously design a business model that prioritises hustle over sustainability. She reinvests everything, avoids drawing a salary, and builds systems that depend on her perpetual presence. To the outside world, she appears industrious. But internally, she is replaying a script: *I can only succeed if I'm the hardest worker in the room.* Another founder, raised in a family where wealth was associated with arrogance or exploitation, may keep the company small, avoid marketing aggressively, or self-sabotage growth—convinced, without realising it, that expansion equals ethical compromise. Again, the narrative is not visible on the balance sheet. But it is embedded in every decision.

Even career transitions—moving industries, going freelance, stepping into leadership—are often shaped more by inherited logic than strategic fit. A person considering a pivot may delay indefinitely, not because of timing but because of a script that says *"you don't get to start over."* Another may change roles compulsively, chasing novelty while avoiding the vulnerability of depth or mastery. Some professionals resist formal leadership because they equate power with moral danger; others rush into it because they believe that status is the only antidote to invisibility. What looks like ambition, avoidance, or indecision on the outside is often the script asserting itself.

There is, of course, a significant difference between reacting to a script and rewriting it. To do the latter requires a level of internal literacy that few workplaces teach. It involves pausing long enough to notice the pattern, then asking a more dangerous question: *What belief is this behaviour protecting?* The undercharging consultant might discover a story about not being smart enough. The over-working manager might realise she's still trying to impress a parent who hasn't been watching for years. The entrepreneur scaling prematurely might be trying to outrun the fear that she isn't good enough without revenue growth to prove it. These are not business problems. They are belief problems. And until they are named, they cannot be re-authored.

The path forward is not to dismiss these scripts—they were often adaptive, even wise, in the original context. The problem is that they rarely update themselves. The consultant *is* now highly skilled. The manager *has* proven herself. The entrepreneur *can* grow at a pace that honours both value and values. But scripts operate like legacy software—they run unless deliberately revised. And in the absence of reflection, we confuse the familiar for the true.

To work script-consciously in a professional context is to bring curiosity, not contempt, to our defaults. It is to examine the rules we've been living by—not to abandon them wholesale, but to ask whether they still serve. It might mean choosing to negotiate a higher rate, not to extract more, but to disrupt the belief that comfort is suspect. It might mean allowing visibility to feel uncomfortable, and still choosing it, as a commitment to contribution. It might mean saying no to the next project—not out of fear, but as a declaration that worth is not tied to workload.

Ultimately, money scripts are not confined to our private financial lives. They are animated, daily, in our careers—through the decisions we make, the chances we take, the recognition we allow, and the patterns we protect. They live in the spaces between emails sent and avoided, meetings dominated or deferred, invoices underpriced or not sent at all. *To rewrite them is not just to change your financial outcomes—it is to reclaim authorship over your professional identity.* And that may be the most valuable currency of all.

Under-Earning and Over-Working

The most destructive financial patterns are often dressed in virtues: hard work, humility, sacrifice, and service. Many people who under-earn and over-work appear, from the outside, to be conscientious and driven. They arrive early, stay late, and say yes when others hesitate. They are praised for their reliability, for being "team players," for going the extra mile. Yet beneath the surface of this competence often lies a set of inherited beliefs so entrenched they are mistaken for personality. One of the most common? *"I have to prove I'm worth it."* Another, equally corrosive: *"Ease is indulgent. If I'm not struggling, I'm doing something wrong."* These aren't abstract sentiments. They are scripts—internalised codes—quietly running in the background of careers, businesses, and bank balances. And until they are surfaced and examined, they continue to write the story.

Under-earning is not merely about income. It is about a mismatch between contribution and compensation, where the value someone brings consistently exceeds what they allow themselves to receive in return. This is rarely due to incompetence. It is often found in highly skilled professionals—therapists, designers, educators, consultants—whose fees don't reflect the depth of their work. Some rationalise it as market conditions. Others say they're "not in it for the money." But probe deeper and a more emotionally charged rationale emerges: *"I don't want to be greedy." "I'm not ready to raise my rates." "I'm afraid they'll leave."* At its core, under-earning is often the behavioural signature of unresolved guilt, fear, or internalised shame about asking for more.

Over-working tends to be its behavioural twin. While under-earning is about the restriction of receiving, over-working is about the compulsion to give—to produce, perform, perfect—usually in ways that exceed what is necessary, recognised, or sustainable. It stems from a core belief that effort equals legitimacy. One must *prove* their right to belong, to be paid, to be respected. Rest becomes suspect. Delegation feels lazy. Ease is equated with moral failure. This belief may have been modelled in childhood by caregivers who were always tired, or in cultural messages that glorify busyness as virtue. The result is a chronic inner stance of *earning your keep*—not once, but continually.

Taken together, under-earning and over-working are not simply bad habits; they are often moral stances inherited from formative environments. In many families, particularly those shaped by hardship, success was permitted only when accompanied by visible toil. You could have "enough," but not more. You could be good at what you did, but not "too" proud of it. You could receive, but only after proving your struggle. These scripts become embedded not as ideas but as truths—emotional facts that structure perception. So, when a professional begins to earn with less effort, or gets paid more than a parent ever did, or receives accolades without working overtime, they may experience discomfort, self-sabotage, or inexplicable guilt. *The issue is not the result. It is the inner breach of loyalty to the script.*

This is especially evident in helping professions. Consider the social worker who avoids private sector opportunities because she associates profit with betrayal. Or the therapist who charges less than market rate because she equates accessibility with virtue. Or the freelance writer who consistently over-delivers on scope because she feels "lucky to be hired." These choices may look altruistic, but they are often fuelled by inherited scarcity and a covert contract: *I will not ask for more, and in exchange, I remain safe from judgement, resentment, or abandonment.* That contract is never explicitly signed, but it governs with the power of law.

Even in entrepreneurial contexts, where earning potential is technically unlimited, many founders replicate the same limitations. A coach launches a programme but underprices it because charging more would require visibility she's not emotionally prepared to hold. A creative professional says yes to every client, despite burnout, because their worth feels proportional to output. A founder avoids hiring because letting go of control means confronting the fear that others might not need her. In each of these cases, the business isn't failing because of poor strategy—it is faithfully executing a script: *"I must be indispensable, exhausted, and undercompensated to be legitimate."*

Ironically, systems often reward these patterns in the short term. The under-earning employee gets praised for "doing it for the mission." The over-working manager receives accolades for "going above and beyond." But the long-term cost is erosion—of energy, of earning capacity, of self-respect. Chronic over-functioning can create resentment, while under-earning limits agency and narrows future choices. Even worse, these patterns become identity-reinforcing. The more someone lives out their script, the more "true" it feels. A person begins to believe they are the kind who must hustle, who isn't cut out for more, who is "just not that good with money." This is not humility. It is internalised restriction masquerading as modesty.

Importantly, these dynamics are not limited to low-paying professions. High earners also under-earn—relative to their value, their peers, or their potential. A lawyer who never renegotiates fees, a tech professional who avoids equity conversations, a consultant who resents their clients but won't raise rates—each of these may be earning well by external standards, but far below what their contribution justifies. In these cases, the under-earning is often accompanied by over-working, which is used to justify the static compensation: *"I don't mind not making more because I get to work with great people." "It's okay because I have autonomy."* These rationalisations are not invalid. But when they become habitual defences, they prevent critical examination. *Am I choosing this, or am I protecting myself from the discomfort of asking for more?*

There are, of course, cultural and systemic forces that shape these patterns—gender norms, class conditioning, racialised economic expectations, and institutional power dynamics. Women, for instance, are socialised to prioritise relationship over assertion, to be agreeable rather than direct, to be grateful instead of ambitious. In such contexts, scripts around earning and working are not just personal—they are socially reinforced. But personalisation still matters. Systems constrain options, but scripts determine which of those options feel psychologically safe. Understanding your script does not eliminate external bias. It does, however, give you leverage to navigate it more strategically.

So what interrupts these patterns? Awareness is the first step, but it is not sufficient. Many people intellectually recognise their tendencies but remain trapped in them emotionally. What's required is a script revision that decouples worth from struggle. This does not mean abandoning effort, but reclaiming it as a choice, not a condition for love, legitimacy, or financial survival. It means asking provocative questions: *What am I proving, and to whom? What would change if I believed that enough is enough—even when I haven't collapsed from exhaustion? Who taught me that being well-compensated is suspect?*

One powerful intervention is to practise earning more *with less drama*. This might mean raising fees without apology, taking Fridays off without over-explaining, or declining extra assignments without guilt. It might involve investing in support—an assistant, a coach, a therapist—to remind the nervous system that ease is not the same as laziness. Over time, these small acts recalibrate the internal barometer. The script begins to update: *"I am allowed to be well-paid and well-rested." "Effort is not proof of value." "Money can come without martyrdom."*

None of this is about entitlement or delusion. It is about recognising that the patterns we assume are personal flaws are often inherited protections. Under-earning and over-working may have kept us safe—emotionally, relationally, or culturally. But safety is not the same as freedom. To earn in alignment with your worth, and to work in alignment with your wellbeing, is not indulgence. It is integrity. And it begins by refusing to rehearse scripts that were never truly yours to begin with.

Scarcity vs. Expansion in Business Behavior

Many entrepreneurs launch their ventures seeking freedom—creative, financial, or structural. They leave traditional employment to set their own terms, imagining a more empowered, abundant life. Yet within a year, many find themselves overwhelmed, underpaid, and trapped by the very systems they designed. They've replaced the office with their home, the boss with the client, the clock with an endless to-do list. The underlying issue isn't strategy or execution. It is the unconscious importation of a scarcity script: *there is never enough—time, money, support, or permission*. Instead of building their businesses from a place of internal expansion, founders often replicate the deprivation they hoped to escape.

At the heart of this pattern is a psychological paradox: we are more likely to repeat the environments we know, even if we dislike them, than to risk constructing ones we can't yet imagine feeling safe in. For someone raised in a household where success was tightly rationed or earned only through exhaustion, spaciousness can feel disorienting. When your inherited money script equates ease with danger or growth with loss, every business decision becomes a negotiation between survival and permission. A freelancer may have the technical skill to double their income but feel an invisible ceiling when they try to raise their rates. A consultant may resist hiring help, not because of cash flow, but because deep down, they believe *"I have to do it all myself."* In each case, the business is shaped more by the founder's emotional inheritance than by their business acumen.

Scarcity-based behaviour in entrepreneurship rarely announces itself directly. It shows up as chronic over-delivery, undercharging, or reluctance to market one's work. It's the designer who revises endlessly without charging extra, the coach who fears being "too salesy," the agency that keeps taking on clients it has outgrown. These are not just operational decisions; they are identity enactments. The business becomes a stage where core beliefs about value, worthiness, and boundaries are continually rehearsed. *What we believe we're allowed to have sets the limits of what we build.*

This is particularly acute in founders who grew up in economically anxious environments. For them, money is not neutral—it is charged, elusive, conditional. They may over-identify with clients' budget constraints, avoid enforcing boundaries, or confuse generosity with depletion. Others may internalise a moral hierarchy, believing that financial success must be justified through service, sacrifice, or social impact. These are often the founders most admired for their integrity—and most likely to burn out. Their businesses are sustained not by sustainable models, but by invisible contracts: *If I do enough for others, I will eventually be safe.* That contract is rarely fulfilled, because the scarcity script it's built on can't deliver a feeling of sufficiency.

Expansion-oriented behaviour, by contrast, operates on an entirely different emotional logic. It doesn't mean reckless scaling, nor does it equate to constant growth. Rather, it begins with a core belief: *"There is enough—and I am enough."* Founders operating from expansion don't wait for proof of safety before they act. They understand that sustainable growth requires boundaries as much as ambition. They invest in help not only to increase capacity, but to honour their own limits. They are willing to be seen—not because they crave attention, but because visibility is not a threat to their identity.

Expansion, at its core, is the willingness to inhabit your full professional stature without apology.

But to operate from expansion, one must first identify where scarcity is driving the bus. For example, a founder may insist on doing all client delivery themselves, citing quality control. But dig deeper, and the underlying script might be: *"If I'm not doing everything, I'm not valuable."* Another might avoid raising prices, not because the market won't bear it, but because they feel guilty earning more than their parents ever did. Or they fear alienating clients who remind them of people they once needed approval from. These emotional entanglements are rarely conscious, but they shape key business decisions—pricing, hiring, marketing, capacity, and even exit strategy.

There are also structural consequences. Businesses built on scarcity often become brittle. They rely too heavily on the founder, resist delegation, and avoid reinvestment. Marketing becomes reactive. Innovation stalls. The business becomes a job with overhead. In contrast, businesses rooted in expansion tend to build for durability. They assume that systems can support growth, that rest is strategic, and that money can be a source of stability rather than stress. These businesses are not necessarily bigger, but they are freer—because their architecture is aligned with a psychology of sufficiency.

The shift from scarcity to expansion is not a branding exercise or a mindset hack. It is a rewiring of deep emotional defaults. One key step is to ask: *What am I protecting myself from by keeping my business small, busy, or under-resourced?* Often, the answers are revealing. *"I don't want to be judged." "I don't want to surpass my partner." "I'm afraid of becoming greedy."* These are not business concerns; they are identity conflicts. And until they are addressed, they will override even the most strategic plans.

Another shift involves creating structures that reflect sufficiency rather than scarcity. This might mean standardising onboarding instead of customising every engagement. Or defining a clear scope of work rather than leaving everything open-ended. It might mean saying no to projects that no longer fit, even if the money is tempting. Each of these is a behavioural vote for expansion: *I trust that clarity will serve me better than control. I trust that alignment is more valuable than appeasement.*

Expansion also means updating relational scripts. Founders operating from scarcity often believe they must be everything to everyone—mentor, friend, rescuer, perfectionist. These roles are unsustainable. An expansion-oriented business respects emotional boundaries. It allows space for the founder to be a leader, not a saviour. It defines clear roles, acknowledges limitations, and understands that being respected is more useful than being liked. This is not arrogance. It is the maturity of someone who no longer ties their worth to others' approval.

Finally, expansion requires redefining success on your own terms. The scarcity script measures worth by effort, output, and sacrifice. Expansion measures success by integrity, spaciousness, and congruence. It asks not only *what* the business earns, but *how* it earns it—and whether that feels aligned with who the founder is becoming. It's the difference between scaling a business to escape burnout, and growing one that allows for rest without justification.

This shift is not linear. Entrepreneurs often oscillate between scarcity and expansion, especially in times of uncertainty. But each moment of clarity—each time they charge what they're worth, protect their time, or invest in support—reinforces the new script. Over time, the emotional centre of gravity moves from fear to trust, from contraction to coherence. The business begins to feel less like a performance, and more like a structure that honours the full intelligence and vision of its creator.

Entrepreneurship always reveals more than it conceals. It surfaces beliefs about enoughness, identity, authority, and safety. And for those willing to see their business not just as a livelihood, but as a mirror, it offers a profound opportunity: to rewrite inherited scarcity in the language of sufficiency. Not as an affirmation, but as a practice. Not for the sake of appearances, but for the sake of freedom. Not just in business, but in life.

Script-Conscious Earning

Most people think of earning as a straightforward transaction: you do the work, and you get paid. But this assumption ignores the profound psychological scaffolding that governs how we approach our income—what feels "enough," what feels deserved, what feels ambitious but permissible. Financial ambition is never just an economic posture; it is also a deeply encoded narrative of self-worth, moral orientation, familial loyalty, and cultural conditioning. When someone undercharges for their expertise, avoids scaling a business, or resists asking for a raise, it is not always about practical constraints. More often, it reflects an inherited script—one that has long gone unquestioned.

Scripts about money are particularly influential when they operate in the background, quietly shaping what we believe we're allowed to want. These scripts are not inherently rational; they are often derived from early models of virtue, shame, obligation, and fear. A script might sound like, *"You shouldn't want more than you need,"* or *"Money changes people,"* or *"Better to be safe than sorry."* On their face, these may appear like moral guardrails. But when internalised uncritically, they become limits disguised as values. *Script-conscious earning begins with the ability to tell the difference between what's truly aligned with your principles and what's merely inherited constraint.*

Take, for example, the common belief among early-career professionals that hard work must precede reward—often without clear endpoints. This idea is frequently romanticised as grit or hustle, but in reality it can become a licence for chronic under-earning. If you were raised in a family where security was scarce and adult worth was tied to relentless effort, then "ease" might unconsciously register as laziness. When that script runs unexamined, it constrains the very freedom that financial ambition is supposed to offer.

Conversely, others grow up with a script that emphasises visible success as a form of validation—whether to maintain status, prove competence, or avoid being perceived as weak. These individuals may become high earners, but still remain tethered to fear. The need to "never go backwards" can drive overextension, anxiety around visibility, or the inability to pause and reflect on whether one's earnings actually serve a life of value. *In both scenarios, earning decisions are being made in reaction to fear, not in alignment with consciously chosen priorities.*

The move toward script-conscious earning begins by isolating the emotional subtext of your financial behaviours. If you're pricing your services, for instance, ask: What belief do I have about how clients perceive value? Do I believe more expensive means more respect—or more rejection? Do I believe I'll be seen as selfish if I charge what I want? These questions aren't theoretical. They expose the emotional infrastructure beneath supposedly rational economic decisions.

A useful thought experiment is to consider how you'd approach earning if no one you grew up around could see or judge your choices. Would you aim higher, ask for more, or work less? The gap between that imaginary freedom and your actual behaviour is often where inherited loyalty lives. *Many professionals are not under-earning because of market conditions—they're under-earning because of unconscious allegiance to a story about what their role in the economic world is allowed to be.*

Cultural identity further complicates the script. In some communities, financial ambition is viewed with suspicion, associated with betrayal of collective struggle or humility. In others, ambition is so deeply baked into belonging that moderation feels like failure. For first-generation professionals or immigrants, there can be a constant tension between legacy and opportunity—between honouring those who came before and not being limited by the sacrifices they made. The challenge is to earn with integrity while recognising that integrity doesn't have to mean replication. *You can respect where you came from without re-enacting its limitations.*

For entrepreneurs and freelancers, script-conscious earning plays out in pricing, marketing, and growth decisions. Founders might avoid visibility because it feels too self-important, or undercharge because they mistake generosity for undercompensation. A coach might keep rates low to remain "accessible," unaware that this reinforces their own belief that people like them shouldn't be earning more. Even when business logic calls for reinvestment or delegation, an underlying script may insist that *"I must do everything myself to deserve the reward."* Over time, these subtle acts of self-sabotage calcify into structural stagnation.

Aligning earning with values does not mean spiritualising scarcity or rejecting ambition. It means asking whether your money goals actually express the kind of life you want—or if they're compensating for old fears. For some, value-aligned ambition may look like scaling rapidly and earning beyond familial precedent. For others, it may mean maintaining a lean operation that prioritises time over revenue. Either can be script-conscious. The key question is: *Are you expanding because you trust yourself, or because you fear falling behind? Are you staying small because it suits your values, or because you fear visibility or failure?*

Script-conscious earning also demands an honest appraisal of how we perform deservingness. Many professionals over-prepare, over-deliver, or over-apologise before asserting their financial worth. These habits often originate in early childhood dynamics, especially in environments where approval had to be earned or affection felt conditional. As adults, the legacy of this conditioning can show up in pricing paralysis, burnout, or the compulsive need to justify one's success. *You cannot out-earn a script that says you are only worthy when exhausted.*

To rewrite the script, start by surfacing your unspoken rules around money and value. When you notice hesitation around charging more, negotiating a raise, or setting boundaries with clients, ask yourself not just *what am I afraid of losing?* but *whose rules am I still following?* Then interrogate whether those rules still serve your current values, context, and vision. This practice is not about psychological excavation for its own sake—it is about liberating your earning potential from obsolete emotional contracts.

At its core, script-conscious earning is about reclaiming authorship over your economic life. It's not about becoming fearless or hyper-ambitious. It's about making money decisions from a place of clarity rather than inheritance, choice rather than compulsion. It demands that we distinguish between genuine alignment and familiar limitation, between growth that reflects our values and success that just performs them. And it asks us, again and again, to remember that financial freedom is not just about having more—it is about needing less from scripts that no longer define us.

Chapter 9
When You Have "Enough" But It's Still Not Settled

One of the enduring misconceptions in contemporary financial thinking is the belief that wealth, once attained, resolves the anxieties it once masked. That accumulating a certain number of zeros will somehow dissipate unease, and that security, comfort, and freedom will arrive unchallenged. Yet, speak with those who have reached such heights, and you often encounter an undercurrent of tension rather than relief. Financial success may tick every societal box, but it does not automatically quiet the scripts inherited long before the money ever arrived. These scripts do not vanish with abundance; they adapt, disguise themselves, and entrench more deeply.

This chapter begins not with scarcity, but with plenty. With individuals who have "enough"—often far beyond ordinary benchmarks—and yet remain tightly gripping, second-guessing, or compulsively rehearsing contingencies that may never materialise. For them, financial planning is less a tool than a coping mechanism. Savings accounts become fortresses. Philanthropy can shift into performance. Budgets are calibrated less to reality than to the echoes of childhood fear. Money becomes something to manage, but not a source of peace.

The paradox of post-accumulation anxiety lies in its subtlety. Those with visible wealth are socially permitted little room to worry—so their unease often moves underground, surfacing through patterns of control: an inability to rest, an obsessive need to monitor accounts, compulsive frugality, or discomfort with self-directed spending. These behaviours are not personality quirks; they are unresolved emotional legacies enacted upon a stage of apparent success.

Inherited scarcity scripts do not dissolve in the presence of abundance; often, they calcify. A child raised amid financial loss may internalise a perpetual anticipation of shortage, even if they never experience it themselves. A high-achieving professional may harbour the quiet conviction that success is conditional, that any lapse could precipitate collapse. These are not irrational fears; they are encoded memories transmitted through stories, silences, gestures, and family routines. They are operating systems often invisible to their users.

Consider a founder who sells their company for tens of millions yet behaves as if bankruptcy is imminent—monitoring minor expenses obsessively, disputing rounding errors, declining basic comforts. From the outside, it may seem eccentric; from within, existential. Their identity, forged in vigilance and control, interprets even success through the lens of potential reversal.

Such dynamics often ripple through families. One generation may amass wealth, the next inherits it—but without the context, struggle, or scarcity that originally shaped it. Intergenerational tension emerges: heirs may feel guilt or unease around money, sensing unspoken obligations to honour it through restraint or replication. The elder generation may fear that the next will squander what was painstakingly earned. This is not a matter of spreadsheets or legal instruments—it is identity transmission. Money is inherited, yes, but so too is anxiety.

Compounding this is a cultural habit of equating financial literacy with strategy rather than psychology. We learn to optimise portfolios, plan estates, and minimise taxes, but rarely to ask: Whose fear am I carrying? What part of me is still proving something? What would I do with this money if unbound by scripts of survival or virtue? These questions are more than intellectual exercises—they are instruments of liberation.

Even noble intentions, such as philanthropy, can be shadowed by unresolved scripts. Giving may serve to legitimise one's right to wealth, rather than reflect genuine choice. Some delay giving under perfectionistic imperatives; others detach emotionally, uncertain if generosity is authentic or penance. Unexamined is the belief in a "right" way to hold wealth—that moral credibility must precede peace of mind.

Then there are the compulsive savers: individuals who continue to accumulate not from ambition, but from fear that any reduction—even for pleasure or rest—might threaten security. Their caution is rarely explicit, manifesting instead in phrases like "You never know" or "Better safe than sorry." Prudence, on scrutiny, often conceals an older, deeper unease: a conviction that no amount is ever truly enough, because enoughness was never cultivated as an emotional state.

To live beyond inherited scripts is not to live without structure. It does not imply financial recklessness or detachment. Rather, it means acting from awareness, guided by values rather than fear. This is no easy task for those whose financial ascent relied on strict adherence to rules: the self-sacrificers, the rule-followers, the eternally responsible. Loosening the grip can feel like betrayal—of family, of self, of systems that once rewarded caution. Yet true financial maturity is not only the ability to earn, preserve, or give; it is the capacity to feel safe even when not in control.

In practice, this might mean allowing oneself an upgrade previously deemed unattainable, sharing the authentic story of family wealth with children rather than a sanitised version, or investing in alignment rather than mere return. It may also mean confronting the pivotal question: if money no longer serves as safety, what does it serve? This is not a philosophical abstraction; it is a practical realignment of life.

This chapter explores these realities through grounded examples and evidence-based insight. We examine how wealth interacts with emotional history, how intergenerational dynamics encode financial scripts, and what it means to unlearn patterns that have outlived their usefulness. We challenge the notion that money has an endpoint, that peace follows accumulation. Often, the work of financial well-being begins only after material needs are met.

The uncomfortable truth that financial culture seldom addresses is this: having enough does not guarantee feeling enough. Until emotional congruence is achieved, no spreadsheet, estate plan, or portfolio will quiet the underlying fear. Yet, by recognising the scripts we carry—and learning to live beyond them—it becomes possible to access a wealth that is not only external but internal; not merely protective, but generative; not just settled on paper, but settling in spirit.

Wealth Doesn't Erase the Script

A high net worth is not a high-functioning money mindset. While wealth may alter the exterior shape of one's life—larger homes, private education, financial advisers—the architecture of internal belief often remains unchanged. If anything, substantial financial success can deepen, not dissolve, the unconscious scripts that shape a person's emotional relationship to money. For many affluent individuals, the paradox is stark: despite evident security, a persistent sense of financial threat, guilt, or inadequacy clings to their decision-making. They do not merely have money; they are haunted by it.

The deeper truth is this: money amplifies the script, it doesn't replace it. Just as a microphone magnifies a whisper, significant financial success tends to expose and intensify the core beliefs one already holds. If someone believes they must hustle endlessly to be worthy, they may now hustle in designer shoes. If another carries a legacy of scarcity, they may become millionaires who cannot enjoy their wealth, compulsively checking accounts and worrying over hypothetical disasters. These are not logical financial behaviours—they are emotional reflexes disguised as prudence.

One of the most insidious myths in modern life is the assumption that wealth is the solution to financial anxiety. Empirical research tells a different story. A Gallup poll of high-income households found that nearly half of respondents—despite earning well above the national average—reported significant anxiety about money. The anxiety did not stem from immediate needs but from *abstract fears*: a market crash, future health expenses, their children's expectations. The core issue wasn't the bank balance; it was the *belief system* framing it.

There's a psychological term for this pattern: *financial hypervigilance*. It's a form of chronic stress-response rooted not in actual threat but in conditioned fear—often handed down generationally. The child of a Depression-era father may grow up in a materially abundant home but still absorb messages like "money can disappear at any moment," or "you can't trust others with finances." Decades later, that same child—now a successful business owner—may still feel unease when delegating financial tasks or making large purchases. The wealth didn't erase the message; it simply gave the message a more luxurious canvas.

A particularly illuminating example comes from estate attorneys and wealth psychologists who frequently counsel ultra-high-net-worth families. Many of their clients are paralysed not by too little money, but by the question of *how to use it without violating inherited taboos*. One woman, a successful tech entrepreneur, confessed she'd rather donate millions anonymously than accept public recognition—so strong was her inherited script that "good people don't flaunt money." Another client hesitated to pay for home help despite owning several properties outright, citing her father's belief that "only lazy people outsource domestic work."

These are not merely quirks of character. They are *coded loyalties*—unconscious bonds to early figures of authority and their financial philosophies. Wealth can enable new options, but without conscious revision of those scripts, the psychological rules remain. The result is often a haunting contradiction: people who can afford to live freely but feel constantly constrained.

There is also the social mask of wealth to consider. Many high-net-worth individuals feel compelled to perform ease, generosity, or status in accordance with their peer group's values. But beneath the surface, they often remain in conflict. A self-made investor may feel torn between a desire to be generous with family and a fear that doing so will "spoil them." A lawyer who grew up working-class might avoid charging premium rates, feeling it would betray their roots. The external lifestyle changes, but the internal calculus remains stuck in old equations.

It is precisely because these tensions operate beneath the threshold of awareness that they are so persistent. Most affluent individuals do not walk around thinking, *I'm obeying an unconscious script.* Instead, they experience subtle friction: an inexplicable discomfort during financial conversations, a recurring impulse to delay major purchases, a guilt that accompanies any indulgence. Without insight, these emotional cues are misread as prudence or personality when, in fact, they are unexamined inheritance.

This is not a critique of wealth, nor a romanticisation of simplicity. Rather, it is an argument for consciousness. *Wealth is not a corrective for inner conflict—it is a magnifier of it.* If one's financial identity is rooted in fear, guilt, or secrecy, those feelings will not be soothed by another zero in the account. They may, in fact, become louder.

The implications extend beyond individual psychology. Families of wealth often struggle to discuss inheritance or legacy planning—not because the money is in dispute, but because the *meaning* of money is contested. Is wealth a reward to enjoy? A responsibility to steward? A danger to children's character? These are not economic questions; they are narrative ones. And without clarity, they produce silence, tension, or conflict dressed up as logistics.

Even among couples, differing money scripts—exacerbated by newfound wealth—can become fault lines. One partner may feel that success entitles them to ease and reward; the other may feel that comfort breeds complacency. These disagreements are rarely about line items. They are about legitimacy, deservingness, and unspoken emotional codes.

This is where financial coaching, therapy, and intentional dialogue play a crucial role. The work is not to rationalise numbers but to *decode narratives*. When a wealthy client feels anxious about spending, the right question is not "Can you afford it?"—but "What does this spending *mean* to you, and where did that meaning come from?" When a philanthropist hesitates to give, it is not always because they question the charity's worth—it is often because generosity feels emotionally risky, like exposing a vulnerable part of the self.

Those who have navigated these waters successfully often describe a shift not in wealth, but in *relationship to wealth*. They speak of permission—permission to enjoy, to share, to let go. They describe a sense of authorship over their financial story, no longer reacting from inherited reflex but responding with intentionality. They are not trying to rewrite the past, but to stop letting it script the future.

To have wealth and still feel financial fear is not irrational; it is unexamined. The antidote is not more money, but more meaning. And meaning comes from awareness, not accumulation.

For professionals, entrepreneurs, and families with substantial assets, the invitation is clear: don't let financial success obscure emotional inheritance. If the goal is true financial freedom, then liberation must begin not with cash flow, but with consciousness. The numbers may add up—but until the script is confronted, the story remains incomplete.

Financial Insecurity in Disguise

Wealth does not always bring ease. For many, the accumulation of financial resources does not eliminate anxiety—it refocuses it. The outward metrics of financial success—healthy portfolios, rising net worth, well-capitalised businesses—can mask psychological patterns rooted not in abundance but in scarcity. Beneath meticulously balanced spreadsheets or meticulously detailed investment strategies, there often lies a fragile internal architecture of fear: fear of loss, fear of inadequacy, fear of reversal. *This is the paradox of modern financial life: plenty can coexist with panic.*

Compulsive saving, hoarding, or excessive financial control are rarely mere strategies of prudence. More often, they are the downstream consequences of internalised beliefs absorbed long before the money existed. Inherited scripts—often invisible to the person enacting them—whisper that one is never safe, never finished, never quite allowed to rest. A person may reach a level of financial security that would have seemed unthinkable in childhood and yet feel just as exposed as they did in their first underpaid job or modest upbringing. The emotional legacy of scarcity remains preserved, even amplified, by the very structures designed to eliminate it.

This pattern is especially common among first-generation earners, those who have crossed a significant socioeconomic threshold relative to their families of origin. For these individuals, financial anxiety often appears as a form of moral vigilance. Success can become not a source of stability but a site of contradiction: they feel guilt when spending, tension when sharing, and terror at the thought of loss—even if their net worth exceeds the safety margins most people would consider reasonable. What they have is never framed in terms of sufficiency, but of looming fragility. The fear of "going back" is not a strategic motivator; it is an existential shadow. *Their inner economy has not caught up to their external reality.*

This is not a rare phenomenon among high-achievers. Many senior professionals, entrepreneurs, and business owners continue to operate with the vigilance of someone still trying to prove worth. They accumulate, but they do not relax. They budget, but not for pleasure. They plan, but not for joy. In fact, *their relationship with money becomes defined less by possibility and more by pre-emption.* Each spreadsheet becomes a ritual against uncertainty. Each capital reserve becomes a psychological sandbag against the rising tide of imagined disaster.

At the centre of this lies a fundamental confusion between responsibility and fear. Many who over-control their financial lives rationalise it through the lens of stewardship, claiming a desire to "be prepared," "stay smart," or "set a good example." These are valid aims—but they become psychologically costly when they are proxies for unprocessed insecurity. Healthy financial discipline enhances agency; compulsive control diminishes it. When the primary goal of money management is to avoid every possible future loss, the present is hollowed out. What remains is a life lived in economic defence, not expansion.

Consider the case of a self-made executive who, after building a business valued at eight figures, still refuses to outsource basic administrative tasks or invest in time-saving services. Her justification—"I don't need to waste money on things I can do myself"—masks a deeper belief: that comfort is suspicious, that ease signals laziness, that money must always be worked for, never enjoyed. Her decision-making does not flow from current reality but from a loyalty to an internal script inherited from a frugal, survival-focused childhood. *She is not managing wealth; she is managing anxiety in the language of money.*

These dynamics are often reinforced by social feedback loops. People who hoard or save compulsively are rarely challenged for it—instead, they are praised for their restraint, their wisdom, their caution. Unlike overspending, which tends to attract concern or judgment, over-saving or over-controlling finances is culturally endorsed. "You can never be too careful," we say. But the truth is: *you can be too careful.* When caution morphs into rigidity, and prudence eclipses generosity, the financial script has turned pathological. It no longer serves the person—it imprisons them.

Philosophically, this invites a deeper question: what is money for? If it does not yield greater freedom, then what is its function? Many people amass wealth out of an unconscious hope that one day, with "enough," they will finally feel safe. But unless the underlying beliefs about safety, worth, and control are confronted, that day never comes. *Enough is not a number. It is a relationship to money rooted in inner clarity, not external accumulation.* Without that clarity, wealth becomes a recursive loop: the more one has, the more one fears its loss.

This pattern is often passed silently between generations. A child raised in an environment of abundance may still inherit the ambient anxieties of their parents. The message is not spoken outright—it is felt. The parent never talks about money directly, but their actions communicate it: avoid risk, don't trust others, work harder than everyone else. Children absorb this, not as financial advice, but as existential instruction. They come to believe, often without knowing it, that comfort is dangerous, that joy must be earned through toil, and that security is a myth no matter how much sits in the bank. *They inherit the feeling of lack, even when the resources are present.*

There is a distinct irony in the fact that people most anxious about money often have the least reason to be. This does not mean their fear is irrational. It means it is misplaced. Their script is not responding to the world as it is—it is responding to the world as it was, or as it was perceived in early life. They are managing yesterday's conditions through today's tools. That mismatch creates unnecessary strain and distorts financial decision-making in subtle but corrosive ways.

Rewriting this script is not about loosening every budget or indulging in reckless spending. It is about reassessing the emotional assumptions that underpin one's habits. Why, for instance, is the idea of taking a sabbatical terrifying, even when one could afford it ten times over? Why is giving generously a source of unease rather than joy? Why does spending money on beauty, rest, or pleasure feel like a moral failing rather than an expression of aliveness? These questions are not tactical—they are spiritual. *They point to the deepest dimensions of how a person understands worth, safety, and identity.*

Psychologists and financial therapists increasingly recognise that money behaviours do not always reflect financial reality. Rather, they mirror emotional experience. Someone who compulsively saves is often attempting to create externally what they lack internally: a sense of enough. But that feeling cannot be bought, hoarded, or accounted for. It must be developed through conscious engagement with the internal narratives that govern one's economic behaviours. In other words, *healing a scarcity mindset is not a financial task—it is a psychological one.*

This is why financial planning, for all its importance, cannot solve what is fundamentally a belief problem. A well-constructed investment strategy is meaningless if the investor is incapable of enjoying the fruits of their labour. Likewise, a carefully managed estate plan does little to improve a person's quality of life if every spending decision is accompanied by shame, guilt, or dread. Financial tools are only as useful as the emotional architecture that surrounds them.

To live with abundance is not merely to possess wealth—it is to be internally available to it. This requires ongoing inquiry, conscious reflection, and sometimes uncomfortable self-examination. It requires asking whether the behaviours one calls "smart" are actually compulsive. Whether "preparedness" is code for fear. Whether "frugality" is masking shame. These are not easy questions. But they are necessary ones for anyone who wants to ensure that their financial life reflects not their past, but their present.

Abundance begins not with the number in your account, but with your ability to live unburdened by inherited fear. Until that happens, financial insecurity will remain—not as a problem of resources, but as a shadow cast by the scripts we have yet to name.

Intergenerational Financial Anxiety

A child can inherit wealth without inheriting a sense of financial safety. This paradox lies at the heart of intergenerational financial anxiety, a phenomenon that quietly shapes the lives of individuals across class lines, economic systems, and family cultures. What begins as a family's experience of gain or loss often reverberates—emotionally, relationally, and psychologically—long after the original event has passed. Wealth, it turns out, may change the external circumstances, but it rarely rewrites the internal narrative unless that process is made explicit. *In the absence of reflection, fortune's ripple becomes burden's echo.*

There is a tendency to imagine that money, once acquired, solves the problems that a lack of it created. This belief is not just naive—it is structurally flawed. Because money is not merely a resource; it is a carrier of meaning. And meaning, particularly in families, is inherited in invisible ways. When a parent lives through poverty, their behaviours—frugality, caution, defensiveness—may appear rational. But when their child, raised in a context of abundance, adopts the same patterns without context, they transform into shadows. They are no longer survival strategies. They are inherited anxieties with no clear source.

Family stories carry weight, often far more than the bank account. A grandfather who lost everything in the 1930s, a mother who kept all her cash in envelopes after growing up under currency devaluation, an uncle who went bankrupt despite early promise—these narratives are rarely told directly, yet their emotional charge is absorbed. A child learns, without needing to be taught, that money is not to be trusted, that security is always temporary, that success can vanish. Even when this child grows into a professional with a robust income and sophisticated financial tools, the undercurrent remains: *you could lose it all tomorrow.*

This kind of inherited financial anxiety often manifests in behaviours that appear out of sync with reality. A young adult may refuse to invest, not because they lack information, but because they carry an embodied memory—transmitted, not experienced—of markets crashing and homes being lost. A business owner may overwork compulsively, convinced that rest equals risk, despite solid financial footing. A professional may feel intense guilt about raising their rates, even when colleagues with comparable experience do so without hesitation. These are not market-driven decisions; they are memory-driven decisions—only the memory is not their own.

Psychologists studying intergenerational trauma have long noted how unprocessed emotional experiences tend to repeat, often unconsciously, in subsequent generations. Financial experiences are no exception. The trauma of lack—of watching a parent worry over bills, of hearing arguments about debt, of witnessing financial collapse—lodges itself not just in memory, but in behaviour. Even when a family later gains security, the emotional residue lingers. The child who grew up hearing "we can't afford that" at every turn may struggle to feel deserving of even modest luxuries, no matter how much they earn. They internalise a script in which desire is dangerous and ease is suspect.

The inverse is equally complex. A child raised in visible abundance may develop financial anxiety not because of lack, but because of silence. Families who "have enough" often avoid talking about money altogether, as though mentioning it might summon judgment or destabilise identity. In such households, money becomes taboo—a source of power, perhaps, but also of discomfort. Children in these families may sense the tension, the expectations, the coded messages about self-worth and status, without ever being invited into an honest conversation. This creates a vacuum where financial understanding should be. And in that vacuum, anxiety thrives.

In both types of households—those marked by visible scarcity and those marked by concealed wealth—financial narratives become sedimented. They are absorbed through tone, through behaviour, through what is withheld as much as what is said. *What is not processed is passed on.* Without deliberate intervention, the child becomes the next chapter in a story they didn't write but must now live.

This dynamic intensifies during moments of family transition—inheritances, losses, unexpected windfalls, or crises. A family that receives a sudden increase in wealth may experience not ease but fragmentation. Long-suppressed scripts surface. Old rivalries, fears, and questions about worth become amplified. Who deserves what? What does this money mean? Is it safe to spend it? Is it noble to give it away? These are not financial questions. They are existential ones. And unless a family has the tools to navigate them, wealth becomes not a blessing but a burden—a source of stress, avoidance, and fracture.

In families where wealth has been lost, the narrative may become one of permanent vulnerability. Even if subsequent generations rebuild, they may do so with an edge of panic, an urgency that betrays the presence of an invisible adversary: memory. The story of loss becomes mythologised—retold with reverence or dread—and this narrative acts as a constraint on the imagination. *It says: Be careful. Do not trust prosperity. Safety is temporary. You must always be on guard.*

This pattern is observable in families across class boundaries. Among families of modest means, children may grow up feeling ashamed of financial limitations, carrying that shame into adulthood in the form of avoidance or overcompensation. Among affluent families, children may feel overwhelmed by unspoken expectations, leading to paralysis, rebellion, or compulsive performance. In both contexts, the root issue is the same: money has become loaded with emotion, silence, and meaning that was never unpacked.

Breaking this cycle requires more than financial literacy. It requires narrative literacy—the capacity to identify the story you inherited, examine its logic, and decide whether it deserves to continue. This is delicate work. It asks individuals to distinguish between what was true for their parents and what is true for them. It requires one to feel the difference between loyalty and identity. And most importantly, it demands the courage to write a different script, not in defiance of the past, but in dialogue with it.

Such work is not purely introspective. It involves difficult conversations. Families must learn to speak across generations not just about assets and taxes, but about fear, value, and vision. Parents need to articulate not just what they want to pass on, but *why*. Children need to be invited into conversations about stewardship, not just as future beneficiaries, but as participants in meaning-making. The goal is not to eliminate tension, but to name it—so it does not govern in silence.

Some families find support for this work through financial therapy, wealth counselling, or intergenerational planning facilitated by trained professionals. Others begin simply by telling the stories: What did money mean to your grandparents? What did your parents teach—explicitly or implicitly—about success, security, or shame? When did you first feel anxiety around money, and who did it belong to? These questions are not academic. They are the gateway to freedom. Because *when the story is unconscious, it controls you. When it is conscious, you can choose your relationship to it.*

Ultimately, the challenge of intergenerational financial anxiety is not about numbers. It is about integration. It is about learning to live with the past without being bound by it. It is about developing the capacity to feel the weight of inheritance without being crushed by it. And it is about offering the next generation not just wealth, but the emotional clarity to handle it with grace.

There is no guarantee that the future will replicate the past. But unless we examine the stories we've inherited, we will unconsciously recreate them. Whether through overspending or over-saving, through avoidance or hypercontrol, through guilt or grandiosity, we act out what we do not understand. *And understanding begins not with more data, but with a deeper willingness to ask: Whose fear am I carrying? Whose dream? Whose doubt?*

Only then can we begin to reframe what money means—not as a legacy of anxiety, but as a canvas for conscious possibility.

Living Without a Script

Most people navigate their financial lives on autopilot, steered by inherited assumptions so deeply embedded they are rarely examined, let alone challenged. These internal scripts—quiet declarations like *"Success means always having more,"* or *"Spending on myself is selfish"*—act as the silent governors of our money decisions. We don't question them because we don't see them. They masquerade as common sense, prudence, ambition, or even moral virtue. But once recognised for what they are—scripts handed down through family lore, cultural norms, or outdated economic models—they lose their grip. And what comes next is both disorienting and quietly revolutionary: *the opportunity to choose with awareness rather than obligation.*

Living without a financial script does not mean operating without principles. It means that the principles are *chosen*, not inherited. They emerge from clarity rather than compulsion. But this shift is not clean or linear. In fact, it often begins with dissonance: a growing discomfort with the way things have always been done. Perhaps it's a professional who realises that relentless achievement leaves them chronically unsatisfied. Or a saver who begins to suspect that their caution masks something closer to fear than wisdom. The discomfort signals the presence of an outdated map—a script that no longer fits the terrain of one's actual life.

What does it mean to live without that script? Not to abandon structure, but to liberate oneself from unexamined imperatives. It looks like asking: *What do I truly want this money to do? What story am I enacting when I decline that opportunity, undersell my work, or delay taking a meaningful financial risk?* These questions shift the focus from behaviour to belief—from the what to the why.

Consider someone raised in a household that valorised frugality as a moral good. They may find it difficult to spend on anything deemed "non-essential," even when they have more than enough. The script says: *Good people don't waste money.* But who decides what counts as waste? Is investing in art wasteful? Is outsourcing childcare indulgent? A script does not invite these nuances; it enforces a binary. Living without a script means reclaiming the capacity to define value for oneself, and to let that definition evolve.

This process of self-authorship requires the courage to tolerate uncertainty. Scripts offer the illusion of control. They provide easy answers in complex situations: Save this. Spend that. Never do this. Always do that. But complexity is the nature of adult financial life. Should I change careers, start a business, retire early, support my parents, scale my company, take a sabbatical, renegotiate my rates? There is no single correct answer to any of these questions. There is only alignment—between one's financial behaviour and one's evolving values.

For many, that alignment is obscured by noise—both internal and external. Internally, we hear the voices of our parents, mentors, cultures. Externally, we encounter a deluge of financial advice that promises certainty while delivering guilt. *You're not saving enough. You're spending too much. You should be investing more aggressively. You should be buying experiences, not things. You should have a side hustle. You should scale back. You should dream bigger. You should be grateful for what you have.* When you strip away the metrics and marketing, what remains is the real question: *What is enough for me, and how do I know?*

Living without a script does not provide that answer, but it creates the conditions in which the question can be explored with integrity. It is the difference between defaulting and deciding. Between being managed by history and shaping one's future with deliberation.

The psychological challenge of this mode is not trivial. Human beings crave coherence. Scripts offer a tidy narrative: My father worked two jobs, so I must work hard too. We're the kind of family that always gives back. Money is security, and security is the highest good. These stories give identity. To loosen their hold can feel like betrayal—not only of one's upbringing, but of the self one has always known. That is why this work must be done with both compassion and rigour. Compassion for the parts of us that cling to old rules; rigour in refusing to let them run the show.

The freedom that emerges is quiet, but profound. It's the freedom to spend on what matters, rather than hoard for fear of future collapse. To say no to work that drains your energy, even if it pays well. To charge what your services are worth, without justifying every pound. To invest in your health, creativity, or rest—not because a spreadsheet told you to, but because you have recalibrated your internal compass. *You are no longer living to prove or protect; you are living to participate fully in a life you define.*

There are no perfect models for this kind of financial agency, but there are echoes of it in the stories of those who have consciously redesigned their relationships with money. The successful founder who downsizes not out of scarcity but to reclaim time. The lawyer who steps away from partnership because the values of the firm no longer reflect her own. The retiree who gives generously, not because he was told to, but because it reflects a hard-earned trust in sufficiency. These are not scripts—they are choices.

And even then, the process is iterative. Living without a script does not mean you will never act from fear, habit, or inherited beliefs. It means that when you do, you notice. You pause. You ask again: *Whose voice is this? What am I trying to achieve or avoid? What else might be possible if I let go of this story?* These micro-moments of awareness accumulate. They create a new kind of wealth—one measured not in assets, but in agency.

A common misconception is that awareness must lead to radical change. But often, what shifts is not the action but the relationship to it. You may still choose to save aggressively or work long hours or decline an extravagant trip. But you do so from discernment, not compulsion. You are not acting out a script; you are writing a sentence of your own.

This is the essence of maturity: the ability to hold complexity, to honour context, and to act with intentionality even in the absence of guarantees. Financial adulthood, then, is not about arriving at a final destination—it is about developing the muscle to navigate with presence, even in ambiguity. It is not freedom from limits, but freedom from illusion.

Living without a script is not easy. But it is deeply worthwhile. It replaces inherited rigidity with adaptive clarity. It trades obedience for authorship. And it invites us into a relationship with money that reflects who we are becoming—not who we were told to be.

Such a relationship is inherently dynamic. It can't be codified into ten rules or five tips. It asks more of us than compliance; it asks reflection, curiosity, and courage. But what it offers in return is something few financial models can deliver: *a life that feels internally coherent, even when externally unconventional.* A life where money is not the measure of worth, the source of anxiety, or the arbiter of success—but a tool, shaped by conscious hands, in service of chosen values.

Chapter 10
Rewriting Your Financial Identity

By the time many people become aware that their relationship with money is as much psychological as mathematical, they have already spent years following a script they never consciously chose. Choices that felt personal—how much to save, spend, or invest—were often inherited, absorbed through family patterns, cultural norms, or strategies of survival. These invisible instructions shaped reactions to risk, comfort with desire, work habits, and assumptions about what one is allowed to have. The remarkable thing is not that these beliefs exist, but that they operate almost entirely out of sight. To rewrite one's financial identity is to make the invisible visible—and to decide deliberately what to retain and what to retire.

This chapter is not about abstract healing; it is about integration. Awareness is no longer the goal—it is the foundation. What matters now is translating that awareness into a coherent, self-authored life. That process begins with narrative. Before action can change, perception must shift. Not in fragments—here a struggling freelancer, there an over-saver, somewhere in between a tentative investor—but as a whole person, whose past, present, and potential are linked through an evolving money story.

A financial story is more than a chronicle of events; it is an interpretation of meaning, past and future. It traces the line from a childhood of instability to an adulthood defined by chronic under-earning. It highlights how early lessons—like "never owe anyone anything"—manifest as overcontrol, avoidance of collaboration, or resistance to scaling. Most importantly, a money story does more than explain: it liberates. Continuity is preserved without captivity. Conditioning becomes context, and the self becomes author.

For some, this moment comes quietly—a shift in language, a new question in a negotiation, a willingness to say no or yes. For others, the change is dramatic: a career pivot, a long-postponed family conversation, an investment in oneself once thought out of reach. Rewriting a financial identity is not performance; it is fidelity—to values, not inherited fears.

Fidelity does not mean finality. A revised financial identity is not a fixed persona or a branding exercise. It is a living system of beliefs, behaviours, and boundaries that must be practised and adjusted. Insight alone illuminates; it does not rewire. Behaviour does. But the behaviour must be deliberate, reflective, emotionally attuned—allowing for correction without collapse. One does not simply "become" a confident negotiator, a purposeful investor, or a generous giver. One practises becoming them, repeatedly.

To do this, most people need internal filters—decision-making cues translating abstract values into concrete action. Is this choice rooted in fear or alignment? Does it shrink or expand me? Is it loyalty to another's story or commitment to my own? These are not platitudes; they are instruments refined over time, distinguishing regression from recalibration. Old scripts do not vanish—they whisper. A well-honed filter cannot silence them but ensures they are not the only voice in the room.

Once tested, these new patterns begin to stabilise. Yet stability cannot remain private. Financial identity is relational: beliefs are enacted in families, partnerships, teams, communities. Rewriting identity eventually ripples outward—communicating differently, making offers and requests with clarity, refusing to collude

From Money Beliefs to Money Story

Every person has a money story. The tragedy is that few realise they are living one. Fewer still recognise that it can be rewritten. Beneath every transaction, career decision, investment hesitation, or gift given with resentment, there is a quiet but powerful narrative that explains why. It was not composed intentionally. It was absorbed. It formed in kitchen arguments overheard, allowances withheld or dispensed, casual remarks about "those people with money," and birthdays spent counting the cost of joy. What begins as belief—money is scarce, wealth corrupts, hard work is the only virtue—soon becomes behaviour. And behaviour becomes identity. The money story emerges not from conscious authorship but from years of repetition, reinforcement, and emotional imprint.

Yet to move from passive belief to active authorship is one of the most psychologically liberating acts a person can undertake. It is also one of the most exacting. Unlike budgets or spreadsheets, this work is not mechanical—it is interpretive. It demands that a person think of their financial life not just as numbers on a balance sheet, but as a narrative arc shaped by themes, characters, conflicts, and inherited motifs. And as with any powerful narrative, the most compelling stories are the ones that reveal something true—not just about money, but about the meaning attached to it.

For many, the process begins with discomfort. Something doesn't quite fit. The income increases, but the anxiety remains. The savings grow, but so does the guilt. A windfall is received, and instead of joy, there is panic. These contradictions are clues. They point to a dissonance between the present and the past, between outward circumstances and inner scripts. Unexamined money beliefs are like outdated maps—we continue to follow them even when the landscape has changed. *Only when we name the map can we begin to question where it came from and whether it still deserves our trust.*

This is where synthesis begins. Most people already carry fragments of financial insight—realisations drawn from therapy, life events, coaching, or personal reflection. But insight, left unintegrated, has limited power. The real shift occurs when those fragments are arranged into a coherent money story—a narrative that helps the individual understand not only what they learned but *how they learned it, why it stayed, and how it shaped their self-concept.* The story, once named, becomes a site of agency.

Consider a woman who was told from a young age that "you have to work twice as hard to be taken seriously." That belief served her well in certain contexts. It pushed her to excel, to outperform, to achieve. But now, in midlife, it has calcified into something more punishing. Rest feels unsafe. Ease feels indulgent. Even after success, she doubts her legitimacy. Her financial behaviour mirrors this: undercharging, over-delivering, and chronic burnout. Her money story explains not only how she got here, but why change feels threatening. *When a belief has helped you survive, questioning it can feel like betrayal.*

But storytelling, done well, doesn't erase the past—it reframes it. It allows us to honour what was necessary *then* while choosing what is sustainable *now*. A revised money story doesn't mean pretending the old one never existed. It means understanding it so clearly that it no longer has to be repeated.

There is no singular template for a healthy money story. What matters is that it is *authored*, not inherited. That it reflects the individual's actual values, not borrowed ideals. That it makes room for nuance, contradiction, and evolution. A story that allows for generosity *and* boundaries. Ambition *and* rest. Security *and* play. For some, this means recognising that their frugality, once a virtue, has become a barrier to joy. For others, it means seeing how a childhood of scarcity fuels compulsive accumulation even when there is now enough. In every case, the story is not just about money—it's about safety, identity, belonging, and power.

Yet rewriting a money story is not an abstract exercise. It requires a shift in how a person interprets their own experiences. A bad investment is no longer evidence that "I'm bad with money," but an invitation to explore how risk was framed in their early environment. A difficult salary negotiation is no longer a personal failure, but an echo of family scripts around deservingness and shame. *Meaning replaces judgment. Curiosity replaces self-blame.*

This narrative clarity, once established, becomes a foundation for action. When a person knows the story they've been telling themselves, they can begin to tell it differently—first in thought, then in practice. That might look like making financial decisions that would have once felt foreign: asking for more, spending on pleasure, setting limits with family, or allowing money to circulate rather than stagnate. These actions, while practical on the surface, are also narrative interventions. They reinforce the new story. They build the muscle of coherence.

Over time, these choices accumulate into something more durable than change—they become identity. A person starts to see themselves not as the one who must always worry, hustle, or compensate, but as someone who can hold complexity. Someone who is allowed to want. Someone who no longer equates deprivation with virtue. This is not a shift that happens all at once. It is iterative. It deepens with each decision made from authorship rather than autopilot. *And like any good story, it becomes more powerful the more it is told—with integrity, not performance.*

It is tempting, especially for high-functioning individuals, to approach this work as another form of mastery. To want to "fix" the story once and for all. But this approach itself is often part of the script. Control, perfectionism, urgency—these are not values. They are trauma responses in disguise. A money story is not something to be optimised. It is something to be *lived into*. That means allowing for uncertainty, contradiction, and—most radically—ease.

In this sense, the true measure of a rewritten story is not how different it looks, but how *honest* it feels. Does it reflect who you are becoming? Does it make room for your complexity? Does it allow you to hold ambition without punishment, wealth without guilt, and generosity without martyrdom? If so, it is already working. Not because the numbers are perfect, but because the self behind them is no longer split between legacy and desire.

To move from money beliefs to a money story is to choose authorship over inheritance, reflection over repetition, and meaning over mechanics. It is a shift from managing money to relating to it—from seeing it as an external force to recognising it as a narrative medium. Your money story is not your bank account. It is your interpretation of value, power, safety, and worth. It is shaped by the past but not defined by it. And it is yours to revise. Not once, but continually.

The work, then, is not to get the story "right," but to make it *true*—to who you are, what you value, and what you want to build. That is the story worth telling. And retelling. Until it no longer feels like a rewrite, but a return to something more honest than the script you were given: *yourself, in full authorship, finally speaking your own lines.*

Practising New Financial Behaviours

There is a moment—subtle but defining—when someone realises their financial behaviour no longer aligns with who they are becoming. Not because they've read a book or attended a workshop, but because their body resists an old pattern. The impulse to undercharge, over-save, decline pleasure, or delay investment feels off. They pause. That pause is the first behavioural boundary between the inherited script and the authored one. Yet insight, without behaviour, cannot hold. If a revised financial identity is to endure, it must be practised—not just reflected upon. *You do not change your financial story by thinking differently alone; you change it by acting differently, repeatedly, under real-world conditions.*

To practise new financial behaviours is to shift from theory to embodiment. It is to place your values under stress—not in abstraction, but in the friction of choice. A person who decides they are no longer governed by scarcity must learn how to say yes without justification. A person who has reframed their relationship to deservingness must learn how to charge fully, spend guiltlessly, or set limits unapologetically. These are not intuitive acts for someone raised in another script. They are psychological exposures. They create discomfort precisely because they are working. *The discomfort of acting out a new belief is the cost of not reverting to an old one.*

At this point, the central question becomes: how does one build a financial behaviour that reflects a newly chosen narrative? Not as a performance, not as a reaction to the past, but as a sustained practice grounded in clarity, consent, and lived experience. The answer is neither purely psychological nor purely tactical—it lives in the space between. It asks not only *what* you do with money, but *why*, *how*, and *for whom*. True change requires not just financial literacy, but financial literacy anchored in script-awareness.

One of the most practical entry points is the use of *decision-making filters*—not rigid rules, but guiding questions that disrupt autopilot. Before making a purchase, accepting a rate, saying yes to a project, or refusing an opportunity, one might pause to ask:

- Does this choice reflect my current values or my historical fears?

- Am I saying yes to avoid discomfort, guilt, or conflict?

- If I were not trying to prove, rescue, control, or please, what would I choose?

- What belief is this behaviour reinforcing?

These filters do not eliminate emotion, but they introduce intentionality. They transform transactions into sites of self-authorship. The goal is not perfection. It is congruence. Even a "wrong" financial decision can serve as a rehearsal for the new script, if it is made consciously.

Equally vital is the adoption of *small-scale experiments*. Major overhauls—quitting a job, radically restructuring assets, confronting a family financial pattern—may be warranted, but they are rarely the first step. Instead, lasting change emerges through consistent behavioural testing. A client raised with the belief that money should never be spent on non-essentials might start by intentionally buying one high-quality, non-utilitarian object. The point is not the object; it is the psychological resistance that must be met and metabolised. Another individual might set a boundary with a relative who expects financial support, not to be punitive but to practise self-respect in action. *Every action, however small, teaches the nervous system something about safety, agency, and self-trust.*

These experiments matter because financial scripts are not just mental—they are somatic. They live in the body, reinforced by past experience. Practising new behaviours is not about logic alone; it is about increasing one's tolerance for emotional dissonance. Someone who equates wealth with abandonment may feel guilt when earning well. Someone who associates spending with danger may feel anxiety during purchases. These sensations are not signs of failure. They are artefacts of the old script being decommissioned. Naming them as such helps avoid misinterpretation. *Discomfort is not always a warning—it can also be a signal of growth.*

Practising new financial behaviours also requires adjusting the social environment. Scripts are often relational. They were transmitted through family systems, romantic dynamics, workplaces, and cultural groups. As new behaviours take root, old relationships may react. A friend accustomed to co-rumination about financial stress may withdraw when you begin to speak with agency. A partner might resist changes to spending dynamics. A parent may express disapproval when you make choices they wouldn't. These reactions are not evidence that you are wrong; they are reminders of how tightly scripts are bound to belonging. *To practise new financial behaviours is also to rewire your relationship to approval and conflict.*

This is why *community and accountability* are essential. Practising in isolation is possible, but limited. Trusted relationships—whether with a coach, therapist, peer, or partner—can create the reflective scaffolding needed to solidify new scripts. Not every person needs to understand your journey. But at least one person should be able to witness it, remind you of what you've claimed, and reflect back the difference between progress and performance. *Practising alone is brave. Practising with support is sustainable.*

Another critical but often overlooked tool is the use of *language*. The words used to describe money behaviours shape how they are interpreted. Consider the difference between "I'm trying not to overspend" versus "I'm learning to trust that there is enough." Or "I can't afford that" versus "I'm choosing not to allocate my resources there right now." Language either constricts or expands identity. Practising new financial behaviours without revising the language used to describe them is like trying to write a new story using an old vocabulary. Precision matters. So does tone. *Speak about your money like it belongs to the self you're becoming—not the one you're outgrowing.*

Over time, these practices accumulate into new defaults. What once felt forced begins to feel familiar. A person who once checked their bank balance daily out of anxiety may find they now do so weekly out of confidence. A professional who once negotiated contracts from fear of being undercut may now begin from clarity about their value. These shifts are subtle but durable. They are not external achievements; they are internal alignments. *The measure of progress is not just how much you have, but how much you have to contort to keep it.*

Importantly, practising new financial behaviours is not a linear process. Regression is not failure—it is data. Falling back into an old pattern does not erase growth; it highlights what is still unintegrated. A setback is not a verdict; it is a diagnostic tool. Used well, it reveals where the script still holds sway, and where the new story needs reinforcement. *Consistency, not perfection, is the goal.*

Ultimately, the work of practising new financial behaviours is not about managing money. It is about managing meaning. Each behaviour is a vote for the kind of life you believe you are allowed to live. Each decision is a small act of reparenting. Each choice, made with awareness, is a line in a new story being written—not to impress, conform, or protect, but to express. The person you are becoming is not an ideal. It is someone whose values are now legible in their calendar, in their bank account, in their tone of voice, and in their level of ease. Not because the numbers are perfect, but because the narrative is chosen.

This is the essence of practice: not discipline for its own sake, but action aligned with meaning. Practising new financial behaviours is the bridge between insight and identity. And once crossed, it is the path by which the new story becomes not just true in theory—but visible, embodied, and lived.

Building a Script-Conscious Life

There is a distinct difference between insight and integration. To realise that you've inherited limiting beliefs about money is meaningful. To rewrite those beliefs is transformative. But to consistently *live* in accordance with a new script—to allow it to shape the way you earn, relate, spend, give, and plan—is something else entirely. It is the difference between insight as a personal revelation and insight as a public declaration, evidenced through choice and behaviour. *A script-conscious life is not one in which old beliefs are simply replaced, but one in which new beliefs are enacted, tested, and stabilised in the spaces that matter most.*

Living a script-conscious life is not about perfection or enlightenment. It is about choosing awareness over autopilot—especially in the domains where inherited financial scripts tend to replicate themselves most insidiously: our relationships, our work, our giving, and our legacy. These are not abstract categories. They are the crucibles where money beliefs become real—revealed not in what we say we value, but in how we show up when value is on the line.

Take relationships. Financial scripts are rarely more activated than when money intersects with intimacy, obligation, or status. A person raised to equate self-worth with self-sacrifice may struggle to accept generosity without guilt. Someone who was taught that money is a proxy for love may over-give in an attempt to secure affection. A family culture built on frugality may silently punish those who pursue wealth. In all cases, the relational field becomes a mirror—and sometimes a battleground—for financial identity. *To live a script-conscious life in relationship is to name, negotiate, and sometimes disrupt these patterns in service of clarity, mutual respect, and equity.*

This does not mean refusing to share or becoming financially isolated. Rather, it means interrogating what lies beneath the gesture. Is this gift offered from abundance or from obligation?

Is this silence about a shared budget born of privacy or avoidance? Is this resistance to prenups about trust—or a fear of being seen as calculating? Questions like these are not academic. They are essential. *Awareness is not the enemy of intimacy; it is its foundation.* Without it, we risk reproducing our parents' dynamics in a new form—different figures, same formula.

Work, too, is a place where old scripts seek expression. For many, work is not just a means of income, but a proving ground for identity. Beliefs about deserving, worth, safety, and scarcity often surface here first. Someone who has rewritten their internal script to embrace sufficiency may still say yes to underpaid work out of fear of being unchosen. Someone who believes intellectually that rest is not laziness may still fill their calendar compulsively. The body often lags behind the mind. *Script-consciousness in work means catching these micro-moments before they calcify into patterns.* It means declining out of alignment, not reactivity. It means pricing one's work not to appease, but to reflect value honestly. It means defining success in terms chosen consciously, not inherited quietly.

Of course, this becomes more complicated when your new script places you at odds with your field, family, or community. A first-generation professional may feel conflicted about earning far more than their parents ever did. A woman who asserts her rate in a male-dominated industry may be labelled difficult. A person choosing work-life integration over burnout may be judged as unambitious. These frictions are not evidence that the new script is flawed. They are signs that it is real. *When you begin to live differently, others may not know how to respond. Your clarity will feel like conflict to those still living by a code you've left behind.*

This is why giving—and the motivations behind it—must also be re-examined. Conventional philanthropy often reinforces the very power dynamics it claims to redress. Script-conscious giving asks not only *what* you give, but *why*, *to whom*, and *with what expectations*. Is the gift a performance? A strategy for control? A disguised form of self-atonement? Or is it a genuine expression of shared humanity and trust in the recipient's agency? A parent might choose to support an adult child through university. That decision, in and of itself, is neither script-bound nor script-free. What makes it conscious is the presence of dialogue, clarity of intention, and absence of coercion. *Giving is not always generous. It can also be a covert currency for identity maintenance or relationship management.*

To give from a script-conscious place is to disentangle generosity from self-concept. It is to stop using giving as proof of goodness, and instead approach it as a practice of redistribution, dignity, and alignment. This redefinition has implications far beyond charity. It affects how we tip service workers, how we share profits in business, how we talk to our children about inheritance, and how we engage in mutual aid. It challenges the fantasy that we can give without power—and invites us to hold that power with more humility and honesty.

Which brings us, inevitably, to legacy. Legacy is not simply what we leave behind in material terms. It is the emotional and ethical residue of our financial lives—the stories, permissions, and patterns we pass on. Living a script-conscious life means recognising that our legacy begins not when we die, but in how we live. A parent who teaches a child that money is a tool, not a weapon, is already shaping their legacy. An entrepreneur who builds a business based on equitable pay is already shaping their legacy. A person who breaks the silence around family money trauma is already reshaping the arc of inheritance. *To live script-consciously is to interrupt intergenerational cycles—not by rejecting the past, but by refusing to replicate it unexamined.*

And yet, this process is not always clean or linear. Old scripts re-emerge under stress. Integration is recursive. You may find yourself reverting to over-saving during uncertain economic times, or people-pleasing when faced with a financial ask. That is not failure. It is feedback. A script-conscious life is not free of contradiction—it is free of denial. The work is not to eliminate all traces of fear or conditioning, but to respond to them with awareness. *Self-trust is built not through flawless execution, but through repeated repair.*

The final layer of script-consciousness lies in how we narrate it. The stories we tell about our choices shape how we experience them. Saying "I'm cutting back because things are tight" feels different from saying "I'm choosing a more sustainable rhythm right now." Both may involve the same financial behaviour—but only one reflects authorship. The point is not to spin or sanitise. It is to claim. When a person rewrites their script but continues to describe themselves through the lens of deprivation, martyrdom, or fear, the new behaviour will always feel temporary. *A sustainable script must also be a narratable one—something you can speak aloud with coherence and pride.*

Building a script-conscious life, then, is not a project with an endpoint. It is a form of ongoing authorship. It demands both discernment and compassion, both self-awareness and systemic awareness. It requires you to recognise that personal money work is always entangled with cultural, historical, and structural forces—and that personal responsibility must be held in context, not in isolation.

The reward for this work is not ease in the conventional sense. It is depth. It is the ability to meet financial choices not with reflex, but with reflection. It is the capacity to live in congruence with your own values, even when no one else understands them. It is the clarity of knowing that your money, like your time and energy, is now in service of something chosen—not inherited by default. A script-conscious life is not only a financial evolution. It is a psychological liberation. It is the difference between acting out someone else's idea of safety, success, or worth—and defining those terms for yourself, out loud, with full consent.

The End of Inheritance, The Start of Choice

It is tempting to believe that once we recognise the scripts we've inherited—those unconscious financial codes passed down through family culture, historical trauma, or social context—the work is done. Recognition certainly matters. It disrupts the trance of repetition. But insight alone is not liberation. *True authorship begins not with understanding what shaped us, but with choosing what we will allow to continue.* The moment we realise that we can honour where we came from *without* continuing to live by its unspoken rules is the moment choice becomes possible.

This shift is subtle but profound. For many, inherited scripts carry not just behavioural patterns but emotional loyalties—allegiances to the pain, effort, and survival strategies of those who came before. A grandmother who lived through war-time rationing may have passed down a reverence for frugality. A parent who clawed their way out of poverty may communicate, through tone and gesture more than words, that security must be hoarded, not shared. Even abundance can be burdened when it's tethered to old anxieties. And so, when a child or grandchild begins to think differently about earning, spending, or giving, it can feel—not intellectually, but viscerally—like betrayal.

But what if growth doesn't require disloyalty? What if it is, in fact, the highest form of honour to evolve the legacy we've inherited—to preserve its wisdom while discarding what no longer fits the conditions of our lives? *Financial reparenting is the conscious act of doing for ourselves what our early context could not: offering permission, correction, and care where old patterns still dominate.*

Consider someone who was raised with a deep fear of financial instability. That fear might have propelled them to earn aggressively, to save compulsively, or to avoid financial risk even when well-resourced. These behaviours might appear responsible or prudent from the outside. But inside, they are often driven not by vision, but by vigilance. Reparenting here might look like learning to trust sufficiency. It might mean giving oneself permission to rest, to spend without guilt, to invest in enjoyment rather than just endurance. None of this erases the wisdom embedded in earlier survival strategies—it simply updates them for the present. *You are allowed to outgrow what once protected you. That is not abandonment. That is continuity with intelligence.*

This is especially important when navigating the emotional terrain of familial financial change. When someone becomes the first in their family to break through an income threshold, purchase property, or acquire assets, they often encounter a quiet ambivalence—pride laced with resentment, love punctuated by caution. The script says: "Don't forget where you came from." The unspoken addendum is often: "And don't act like you're better than us." But growth is not superiority. It is a shift in context, in resources, and in possibility. Those who learn to carry their history without being confined by it offer their family something more enduring than sameness: *they offer evidence that transformation is possible.*

Financial reparenting, then, is not merely internal. It affects how we engage with others. It alters our communication, our generosity, and our boundary-setting. Someone who grew up around secrecy may choose to practice transparent conversations about money. Someone raised with control may learn to share decision-making. Someone whose family equated spending with irresponsibility may learn to embrace pleasure without shame. These are not abstract ideals. They are behavioural shifts rooted in self-trust. And self-trust is cumulative—it is built through small, repeated acts of alignment.

But choice, as a concept, is easy to romanticise. In practice, it often feels disorienting. The moment we stop following a script, we lose the certainty that comes with external validation. There is no longer a prescribed role to play. You are no longer "the saver," "the martyr," "the striver," "the generous one." You are simply you, responding to context, values, and desire in real time. *This kind of authorship is vulnerable. It requires the courage to live without templates.*

It also requires tolerance for tension. There will be moments when new choices provoke old guilt. There will be holidays where spending differently from your siblings brings discomfort. There will be investment decisions that clash with the ethos you were raised with. In these moments, the goal is not to eliminate discomfort, but to meet it with discernment. Ask: *Is this discomfort the result of misalignment—or of growth?* The former requires adjustment. The latter deserves applause.

This tension is nowhere more evident than in legacy work. What do we pass on? What values, structures, or assets do we embed into the next generation? Too often, people think of legacy in purely material terms—wills, trusts, estates. But legacy begins much earlier. It is shaped in how we talk about money, in the permissions we grant, in the scripts we consciously dismantle. A script-bound legacy might teach children that wealth must be hidden, feared, or flaunted. A script-conscious legacy teaches discernment: when to conserve, when to share, when to risk, when to rest.

And crucially, legacy is shaped not just by what we say, but by what we model. A parent who says "Money doesn't define you" but panics every time a job is lost transmits a different message than intended. A leader who preaches abundance but hoards resources transmits scarcity through action. Integrity here is not perfection—it is *coherence*. It is the effort to align our internal beliefs with our external behaviours, especially when the stakes are high.

This is where financial reparenting becomes generative. It's not just about healing the past. It's about expanding what's possible in the present. It means choosing not to replicate fear just because it is familiar. It means giving the next generation tools to think critically, not just obediently. It means creating environments—whether in families, communities, or organisations—where money becomes a topic of curiosity, not shame; of strategy, not silence.

To reach the end of inheritance is not to discard what came before. It is to step out of automaticity. It is to stop enacting scripts we never chose and start evaluating which principles, beliefs, and practices deserve to move forward with us. The start of choice is not the start of control. It is the start of *agency*—the willingness to ask, over and over: "What is mine to keep? What is mine to change? What is mine to imagine anew?"

And this is the enduring gift of script-conscious financial work: it returns authorship to the individual without denying the impact of systems, structures, and lineage. It allows us to respect our history without being ruled by it. It teaches us to name the forces that shaped us, but not to confuse them with fate. And in doing so, it opens a different kind of inheritance—one not defined by assets, narratives, or trauma, but by possibility.

We do not owe our past our repetition. We owe it our attention, our compassion, and, when needed, our refusal. Growth is not disloyalty. It is the most sincere form of gratitude—to take what was given, examine it with care, and decide what is worthy of continuation. *The end of inheritance is not a rejection. It is a reclamation. And with it, the start of choice becomes not just a personal evolution, but a cultural shift—one lived decision at a time.*

About the Author

Mira Ellison writes at the intersection of psychology, money, and personal meaning. With a background in behavioral inquiry and narrative work, her writing reflects a deep curiosity about why we repeat the patterns we do—and how to outgrow them with clarity and self-respect. Her work is rooted in the belief that our financial lives are emotional biographies in disguise, shaped by inheritance more than intention. Mira's mission is to help people re-author their internal money narratives without shame or shortcuts. She lives simply, asks big questions, and invites readers to do the same—starting with their most private habits and unspoken beliefs.

www.ingramcontent.com/pod-product-compliance
Lightning Source LLC
Chambersburg PA
CBHW031344230926
51848CB00002B/372